Wonderful Magical Words That Work

Wonderful Magical Wisdom That Works

Perfect gifts — for charity and for those you care about — family and friends, co-workers and clients.

Every book sold benefits Make-A-Wish Foundation — granting wishes to children diagnosed with life-threatening illnesses.

Books are available directly from the publisher — ordering information is at the back of the book.

Here's a sample of how Bill Arnott's books and seminars are making a difference:

BILL ARNOTT'S BOOKS:

"A great book."

> — JACK CANFIELD, BESTSELLING CO-AUTHOR
> OF *CHICKEN SOUP FOR THE SOUL*

"This is a wonderful book full of wonderful words for a wonderful cause. Read it and enjoy!"

> — BRIAN TRACY, BESTSELLING AUTHOR OF *MAXIMUM ACHIEVEMENT* AND *SUCCESS IS A JOURNEY*

"Bill Arnott's *Wonderful Magical Words That Work* really does work. This simple, effective book reminds us of the deep wisdom we have within if we will just tap into it. The 'secrets' Bill shares will guide you along life's journey with increased purpose, joy and meaning."

> — DAVID IRVINE, BESTSELLING AUTHOR
> OF *SIMPLE LIVING IN A COMPLEX WORLD:
> A GUIDE TO BALANCING LIFE'S ACHIEVEMENTS* AND
> *BECOMING REAL: JOURNEY TO AUTHENTICITY*

"Bill Arnott's books help us to understand the importance of words to shape our success and significance. A very good read."

"If you want to move from where you are to someplace better, Bill's books can help you do that. Don't JUST read them — USE them and you will see better results and more peace and satisfaction in your life."

"We can be impressed in our heads by 'wonderful' words and they may motivate us for a short while, however, when words, 'full of wonder', make an impression on our hearts they can inspire us to live life fully forever. Words will quickly turn to dust if we don't take action. Through Bill's profound books, he guides us back to our hearts, full of joy, that we have, too often, forgotten. They are not books we passively read to simply learn more, but books where we will experience more, and feel more passion, meaning, and 'life' in the gift we've all been given... our lives."

"In Bill's books, every passage I read touches my heart and makes me want to share his message with everyone I speak to."

"God bless you in all that you are doing."

"Your book came to me at just the right time and I LOVE it. It was a refreshing read and reminder to me to keep things simple in life. Life is simple, yet we spend so much time making it complicated. Your book helped me to see that yes, indeed, it is simple if you just stick to the basics. Thank you so much."

"I gave [Bill's books] as Christmas gifts to my sister and two of my best friends. Keep up the wonderful work. It's people like you who make a big difference in this world."

— VIDA JURCIC, VANCOUVER

"Hi Bill. You don't know me but my friend gave me your autographed book for my birthday. I've been reading it and I find it simply amazing; inspirational, motivational, and very realistic. I've been mesmerized by the content; it IS a hard book to put down. Thank you so much for sharing your wisdom, your passion and your compassion."

— MEGAN KENNEDY, WHITE ROCK

"I started reading your book and I feel a lot more relaxed already. I will share the book with others. Nice to see [someone] making a difference."

— ED MILITZER, WHITE ROCK

"Thanks so much. Your book's been a real pleasure to read. What a treat! A truly wonderful experience— thank you!"

— ROBIN MCINNIS, VANCOUVER

"Bill Arnott's book has something for everyone. It is a great book that you can pick up at anytime when you need a lift or just a positive thought to start the day. I have given a copy to each member on my team to keep them motivated. It certainly has worked for me."

— HILARY CASSADY, SINGAPORE

"I feel empowered by what you said in your book. Thank you for writing the book. I'm sure many lives will be changed by it (including ours)."

— JEDHA HOLMES, GIBSONS

"[My husband] has terminal cancer and our life has not been as I imagined it would. Over the past four years I have gone through many stages of sorrow, anger and remorse. At times my life was almost consumed with these feelings. I was very stressed last Christmas with thoughts of his deteriorating condition and family visits. Then, your book arrived. Reading *Wonderful Magical Words That Work* was a spiritual awakening for me. It was a wake up call — reminding me that the true joys of life are spiritual, and that we are never alone."

— BETTY GILBERT, SURREY

"Just finished reading [your book] and loved it — thank you for putting into words how many of us aspire to live our lives. The world will be better because people will read your words and start living their dreams! Thank you!"

BILL ARNOTT'S SEMINARS:

"Bill's positive energy & outlook on life is contagious and an inspiration. Everyone should be as fortunate as we were to experience his fun & engaging presentation."

"To 'standing room only' crowds, Bill has managed to show his insights on doubling his business while nurturing his personal life in near perfect harmony. He is funny, insightful and most of all, inspirational. One feels a sense of empowerment when he's through. At any cost, he is a must see!"

"I have found Bill very interesting to listen to and passionate about serving ..."

— MURRAY TAYLOR, PRESIDENT AND CEO, INVESTORS GROUP FINANCIAL SERVICES

"I have never met someone who is as positive and enlightening as you!"

— CHARMAINE MCNEIL, SURREY

"Bill speaks in an intelligent and thought provoking manner that keeps you engaged and entertained at the same time."

— ROBERT O'KEEFE, SENIOR VICE-PRESIDENT, INVESTORS GROUP FINANCIAL SERVICES

"Your presentation put a smile on my face! I felt a warm glow of happiness and felt my power from within and then I looked around the room and saw the same glow from my fellow Rotarians. Then I realized the power that emanated from the group and it all started that morning with us and you. It was amazingly simple!"

— ROBERT MADSEN, PRESIDENT, ROTARY CLUB OF STEVESTON

"Bill exudes enthusiasm and passion in his presentation. He is lively, entertaining and generates an enthusiastic response from his audience. We really appreciate Bill's contribution."

— BRIAN PROCHNICKI, NANAIMO

"You have touched many lives in this small northern community of Thunder Bay. Your positive message has resonated not only through the office but to our clients and families as well."

— EMEY HENDRICKS, THUNDER BAY

"Your confidence in yourself & what you do for people is infectious."

— BEN CAMPBELL, WINNIPEG

"Thank you very much Bill. Your outlook on life is very refreshing and I am glad you are sharing it with others as it does make a difference."

— RENEE WILKINS, BURNABY

"I found [your presentation] very inspiring."

— GLENN MARR, WINNIPEG

"Bill Arnott impacted our team significantly with his inspirational presentation and his words were 'wonderful and magical"! It is refreshing to hear a speaker that has an approach that relates to working on the inner self versus starting with business and outside issues. My team thoroughly enjoyed Bill's session. Bill, thank you for contributing and impacting our team and I know that others will significantly benefit from your message!"

— BALA NAIDOO, BURNABY

"Your discussion was impacting and has got my mind thinking a little differently, which feels great."

— VIVIAN KERR, BURNABY

"Bill, thank you for everything that you did. It really is something to hear great people speak. You really had a fresh perspective that I really can relate to and deeply respect. Once again, thank you so much, it was truly fantastic."

— MICHAEL PRETO, VANCOUVER

To Ian

WONDERFUL
MAGICAL
WORDS
THAT WORK

*Secrets to Create
Permanent Success
and Happiness*

Live your dreams!

- / 3·4

WONDERFUL MAGICAL WORDS THAT WORK

SECRETS TO CREATE
PERMANENT SUCCESS AND HAPPINESS

BILL ARNOTT

WONDERFUL MAGICAL PUBLICATIONS

Canadian Cataloguing in Publication Data
Legal deposit number 881178

Arnott, Bill
Wonderful magical words that work:
secrets to create permanent success and happiness

ISBN: 0-9736350-0-2
First Edition
10 9 8 7 6 5 4 3 2 1

Published by:
Wonderful Magical Publications
White Rock, BC
Canada
(604)542-4331
www.wonderfulmagicalwords.com

Printed in Canada
Printed and bound by Just Your Type Graphics
Book and cover design by Stu Ross

To Debbie
For loving and knowing

"Your words are the outpouring of your consciousness. If you want to know what you really believe, listen to your words. Nothing can change until your words change."

— *JACK BOLAND*

ACKNOWLEDGEMENTS

I would like to express my sincere thanks to my closest friends who were the first to read this book: Trevor Biggs, Brad Campbell, Steve Vanagas, Hilary Cassady and Brent Musico. I greatly appreciate your honest feedback and the time and effort that you gave to me. I thank you for believing not only in me, but in the wonder, the magic, and the power contained in this book and its words.

I would like to thank Wanda Styles and Stu Ross for helping me create this book, and Jeanne Ainslie for her care and enthusiasm in editing this book and providing me with invaluable direction.

And I would also like to express my gratitude to my loving wife, Deb, and to my family; Mom, Dad, Bobbie and Susie for giving me unconditional love. Your loving support throughout my life gave me the confidence and courage to share my feelings and my passion with the world. Thank you.

CONTENTS

WHAT DOES THIS BOOK HAVE TO OFFER?

Do you want more out of life? Do you want to realise your true potential? Do you want greater success and happiness? Do you want to discover the clarity, direction and inspiration to improve every part of your life? If so, then this book is for you! *Wonderful Magical Words That Work* will reveal the secrets to create permanent happiness and success in your life and the lives of those you love.

HOW DOES THIS BOOK DO THAT?

Wonderful Magical Words That Work provides inspirational, life-changing thoughts and insights. By repeating the powerful thoughts to yourself on a regular basis, and making them a part of who you are, you will release the magic they contain. The magic of these thoughts will permeate all you do, generating more goodness, happiness, success and abundance into your life. It will happen immediately for some and over time for others, but by believing in *Wonderful Magical Words That Work*, you cannot help but improve your life. As surely as the laws of nature, you can change who you are, make yourself better, and live a rich life beyond what you may have ever dreamed possible.

These words are a progressive series of motivational thoughts that will enrich your life. Think of it as a disciplined exercise program for your thoughts and behaviour — a healthy diet and strength training for your mind and spirit. Your mind generates all that you have, all that you experience, and all that you are. By training your mind with a regimented program of the positive, opening your channels of creativity and banishing fear and doubt, you can and will redefine who you are and how you live. You will then have the ability to improve the lives of those close to you and ultimately design the life that you want to live.

HOW DO I PUT THIS INTO ACTION?

The fact that you're reading this book shows that you've already made a commitment to yourself. You have invested time, energy and money to get this far. This shows that you have already taken greater initiative than most with respect to self-improvement and creating a better life. Congratulations.

What is critical at this point is to ensure that you maintain your momentum and follow through. You can do this by taking immediate action. Think about where you are and where you want to be; make a conscious choice and implement positive change that will move you consistently closer to your goals and a better life.

At the end of PART 1 — Success From the Inside Out: Focus on You; PART 2 — Sharing Your Success: Focus on Others, and PART 3 — Permanent Rewards: Focus on Life, I present you with an Affirmation Question, which will guide your thoughts towards the positive and initiate a change in your behaviour to improve yourself, your relationships and your life. By reflecting on positive experiences and then answering the Affirmation Question every day, your focus will gradually shift to the positive in your life. This will create a natural, ongoing attraction of more positive in your life like a magnet attracts steel, and positive experiences will perpetuate for you. The Affirmation Question is then followed by a simple Application Exercise. Answer the Affirmation Questions honestly; complete the Application Exercises, and you will significantly increase your ability to improve your life right now.

IMAGINE MY SURPRISE, TO FIND GOD IN MY BMW.
I was between business appointments, and gave myself permission to take a break. Day planner put away, cell phone turned off. The car was parked in a quiet, private parking lot surrounded by trees. I opened the windows and sunroof. The air was fresh. It was spring, but the sun was hot like the middle of summer. I rarely took a break like this. I had been working hard at my career for several years, making good money, and had received a number of national awards from my company. I was thoroughly dissatisfied.

I hungered for something more. The fancy car wasn't enough. The recognition at work felt hollow. I had read hundreds of books on how to be successful and how to find happiness, and yet, peace and spirituality eluded me. I was desperate to find something to rejuvenate me, something to keep me performing at my job, something to make me happy. I had started the practice of meditation, hoping this would give me what I needed. I took advantage of the free time and peaceful setting. I eased the seat back and gazed out the sunroof.

Cotton ball clouds hung there, moving slowly in the sunroof opening like I was watching TV. I relaxed and let my body sink deep into the leather seat. I had heard of the practice of cloud making, but had never tried it. The exercise demonstrates interconnectedness with the world around us. According to the practice, we are able to make actual clouds disappear and appear using our minds. We slip into our environment, lose the belief that we are separate from it, and then create exactly what we wish, in this case, clouds or blue sky. First you see it in your mind's eye, and then you see it manifested into the physical world.

I loved the concept but had doubts. I felt I attained what I had through hard work, determination, and doing good things for people. My world worked on the tangible. But my wife, Deb, and I had recently completed a marathon (26.2 miles), something we had never done before, and it had seemed unfathomable. Now, I was beginning to believe anything was possible.

I focussed on my breathing and relaxed. Clouds continued to hang lazily in my field of vision. I decided to do it; I made a conscious choice. And at that moment, something clicked. For the first time in my life, doubt disappeared. Everything felt within the realm of possibility. I picked out a small, fluffy cloud, closed my eyes and chose to make it vanish. I focussed and visualised myself outside of my physical body. I felt myself extend outside of the vehicle, towards the cloud. I pictured myself breathing in the small white cloud, felt the cool, moist vapour pass across my face and into my nose and mouth. I inhaled and waited.

When I opened my eyes the cloud was still there but visibly smaller and wispier. I shut my eyes again and mentally extended myself back up towards the cloud. I saw myself with a great blue crayon scribbling over the thin cloud, like a child with colouring paper and no lines to follow.

I felt another new sensation as absolute certainty washed over me. I smiled and opened my eyes. The cloud had vanished. I felt an adrenaline surge but trepidation as well. Over the years I had learned to doubt. Belief came conditionally. Maybe it was the years of university, or that statistics course I had to repeat. I needed more observations. How could I create a control group? Clouds are forming and disappearing constantly. What nerve to think that I had anything to do with it. It was ignorant, arrogant and blasphemous. And yet, why shouldn't we be able to do that?

I wanted to be convinced. I found another cloud, slightly larger and denser than the first, and repeated the mental process. Eyes closed, visually extending myself out towards the cloud, breathing it in. I kept my eyes closed and repeated the mental colouring exercise just to be sure. But I knew even before I reopened my eyes. And when I did, the sky was cloudless.

I wanted more. I stared up at the clear blue sky. Closed my eyes, mentally extended and exhaled the same moist air that I had breathed in. I waited for a moment and looked. A fluffy white cloud stood out against the expanse of blue.

It was there. I blinked hard. I looked away and looked back. It was very real. I knew then what I had hoped and believed to be true. I could make clouds. We can make clouds. I repeated the whole process again and again. I was having fun.

Eventually, I stopped the cloud making exercise and closed my eyes. I was ready to conclude my meditation. I listened only to my deep, relaxed breathing. I simply was. I don't know how much time went by, but in my mind I saw a screen open up across my consciousness. It brightened to ivory. Words began to form. The image of words sharpened, scrolling from left to right. TAKE YOURSELF HIGHER.

The words were vivid. I felt immediately connected with creation itself. I held the image, let it fix into my memory. I felt I had found God. This was what I had been looking for all this time. I slowly opened my eyes.

I don't know when it arrived, but there it was, on the hood of my car. Its eyes were sharp and penetrating and fixed onto mine. It was a great black raven, staring at me with a sense of knowing. The moment seemed timeless. It opened its beak and cawed once as it stared at me. Then it spread its wings and flew away.

It took me some time to collect myself, to grasp what I had experienced. Then I felt completely at peace. The sense of awakening was incredible. I felt blissful. I couldn't take the smile off my face.

My joy wavered temporarily when I thought about sharing this. I wanted those I love to know what I knew. To know what we can do. This wasn't about making clouds or being in touch with nature. This was about awareness and potential. This was about our ability to tap into creation and manifest for ourselves exactly what we need, when we need it. It would have been easier to keep it to myself. It was going to take a lot of guts to share this. I would be opening myself up to disbelief and scorn. So be it. I could do it; I needed to in fact. I have no recollection of anything else that happened that afternoon, and it really doesn't matter. I believe I retained all I really need.

I was overwhelmed with a range of emotions that day, from doubt, to wonder and joy. I experienced things for the first time, the power of manifestation and unlimited potential. What had happened to me was an epiphany. I believed that I had made clouds disappear and appear at will. My feelings, emotions and insights were captured in the raven I saw and the words that appeared in my meditation. I can remember what I felt and saw, but the words became part of who I am.

What is important here is that I believed. My belief does not make it true or false. It was true for me in that moment and transformed my thinking from a limiting belief into one without limits, that is, we can do anything.

Since that day, inspirational, life-changing thoughts have continued to come to me in the form of powerful words. These words have changed my life and enabled me to feel thoroughly happy and peaceful. I have enjoyed personal and professional success with remarkable ease as a result of living by the words that have appeared to me through my meditations. I've compiled the words in this book and called them *Wonderful Magical Words That Work*.

I don't feel as though I've written the words. I feel as though I've just written them down. When the words came, they flowed easily and naturally. For this reason I believe that these words have been shared with me, and I am sharing them now with you. They provide direction and affirmation to thoughts and actions many of us would like to experience daily. They have changed my life for the better and they can do the same for you.

Words are thoughts. Thoughts become actions. That is why they work. I know this to be true. But we are only as good as what we give. These words are to be shared. Make the magic a part of your life and the lives of those around you. Use them to give you peace, develop great habits, and construct the life you choose. Use them to help you create all that you want. They work!

This book will enable you to achieve permanent success and happiness in your life. By studying and internalising the *Wonderful Magical Words That Work*, secrets will be revealed to you that will enable you to be happier and healthier, and to have greater success in your work and your relationships. You will have greater abundance in your life and absolute peace of mind. You will first see the magic at work on yourself, then those close to you and ultimately throughout your life.

I wish you all the success and happiness that you desire.

PART ONE	SUCCESS FROM THE INSIDE OUT: FOCUS ON YOU

CHAPTER 1

Making
Yourself
Better

"The golden opportunity you are seeking is in yourself. It is not in your environment; it is not in luck or chance, or the help of others; it is in yourself alone."

— ORISON SWETT MARDEN

"I listened, I was aware of my success, but I never stopped trying to get better."

— MICHAEL JORDAN

"You are the way you are because that's the way you want to be. If you really wanted to be any different, you would be in the process of changing right now."

— ZIG ZIGLAR

TAKE YOURSELF HIGHER

These are the words that changed my life. These words gave me the courage to expect more and to achieve more. Through these words I felt the freedom to look deep into my soul with peace and love and to create what I wanted for myself. You can too.

We are capable of more than we know. But limits are imposed on us. Our family, teachers, the people we work with and society establish these boundaries for us. We come to believe the limits and add to them ourselves. But these limits are fabricated. They aren't real. Once we recognise this, and break down these false limitations, we can see ourselves for our true potential.

Get in touch with who you are. Cast off the ties that hold you back. Recognise all that you can do. Take yourself higher, and live your dreams.

ONLY YOU CAN HOLD YOURSELF BACK.

REALISE YOUR ABILITY TO BE HAPPY, HEALTHY AND SUCCESSFUL

How we feel and what we have is entirely determined by us. Moods don't just happen to us. We make them. Realising our ability to be happy, healthy and successful will be second nature to some and seemingly impossible to others, based on conditioning and beliefs. Separate these words and absorb them slowly and thoughtfully. Don't let these powerful words run together and diminish their significance. You can be happy. You can be healthy. You can succeed. Make the choice. It's up to you.

REALISE YOUR ABILITY TO LOVE

Most of us think of love as something we fall into. I can't think of anything I'd want to fall into. I visualise a pit, a well or a puddle. It doesn't conjure up a positive image. By realising our potential to love, we recognise the fact that love is something we do. It is an action; a choice. If we don't acknowledge this, we won't have love in our lives. As long as we realise our ability to love, we can feel love whenever we choose. Love may or may not be that of a sexual partner or a family unit. Love for the sake of love itself and enjoy the power of love in your life.

FEEL ENTHUSIASM

The word enthusiasm comes from the Greek meaning "God within us". We can live to our potential by living with enthusiasm. Do everything with enthusiasm and enjoy your connection with God.

Physiology follows psychology, but physiology will direct the mind, providing momentum and adding tangible reinforcement to your thoughts. Therefore, behave in a happy and loving manner. Feel love and let your behaviour take on the momentum of this joyful experience. Your mind will embrace this positive energy and create a loving reality.

In our purest state, we are love. Like light, love is the source of everything. Allow yourself to know this. Let it flow over, around and through you. Enjoy the process and feel love.

WE FORGET HOW MAGNIFICENT WE ARE,
EACH AND EVERY ONE OF US.

FEEL GOOD AND STAY HEALTHY

You determine how you feel. It can and will change. That's okay. It's what makes life rich and experiential. Remember your ability to choose. Our physiology is the embodiment of our mentality. We alone control our moods and our behaviour. We can be as happy as we choose to be. We can also be as healthy as we choose to be. I understand that people become sick. Cells in our body can and will mutate, leaving some unscathed while others suffer terminally. However, the documentation of spiritual self-healing is too extensive to be disputed. As the lines separating science and spirituality disappear, we continue to learn fundamental truths. I sincerely feel for those who become ill and for those who suffer. Not everyone is able to succeed in getting healthy. But for those who truly want to feel good, get healthy, and stay healthy, know that you can and will if you so decide. It is absolutely within you.

Like everything in our world, our lives are a perpetual dance. Nothing is constant. This is a wonderful blessing. Everything we enjoy, we know can continue and improve as we go. And for difficulties, challenges and tough times, we can take solace in knowing that they too will change, giving us an opportunity to make different choices, live and behave differently and once again enjoy the dance. Remember your ability to choose. If things feel tough, change them. Choose to make them different and make them better. Enjoy the dance. Be happy and healthy. Stay happy and healthy.

BE GOOD TO YOURSELF AND YOUR BODY

I heard someone say, "Be good to your body. Where else are you going to live?"

We could discuss reincarnation, but I like the concept at its simplest level. The fact is, our bodies are important, but all too often we don't treat them as such. Many of us treat our cars better than we do ourselves. How many people who smoke or overeat put only premium gasoline in their vehicles? These people wouldn't dream of letting the car go too long between check ups, but when was the last time they went to the doctor or exercised? You see my point.

People who put time and effort into maintaining a smooth running engine probably want a nice clean car around it. The same must go for us. Our physiology can make the operation of our mind more effective and it can just as easily work against us. People who are unhappy with their physical selves are most likely to be unhappy, depressed and manifest negativity into their lives. A happy, healthy body can add great momentum to a happy, healthy mind and vice versa. Be good to yourself and take care of this container we call our body, because this is one vehicle you can't easily trade in.

Give yourself time each morning to wake up leisurely. Stretch. Breathe deeply. Give yourself time to just be or to meditate. Decide that your day's going to be exceptional. Know what you'll experience and accomplish for the day. Don't rush. Enjoy the morning. Go about your routine methodically. Contemplate, with pleasure, the simple things you do. Smile, sing and dance a bit. Then have some breakfast, something simple and nutritious. But make sure it's part of your routine.

I can look around our office, identify the most unfit people, and be almost certain that they skip breakfast. Don't fall into the trap of skipping breakfast or thinking you're minimising calories. Your body will hang onto some extra fat it wouldn't otherwise need.

At our office we used to find one of our co-workers regularly in the lunchroom, peeling and eating grapefruit over the sink. He was very likeable. He was overweight. We never saw him eating anything other than the grapefruits. He joked about his weight and his "grapefruit habit". Another co-worker said to him, "That grapefruit must be really fattening." We shared a smile, but then we talked about his food consumption.

Turns out, like many, he was a late night snacker, lots of fatty foods in front of the TV, then off to bed. He'd feel guilty in the morning and skip breakfast, thinking he could compensate for the previous night. The grapefruit kept him going through the day, but by the time he got home in the evening he was ravenous. He'd have a huge dinner and before long the late night snacking would kick in again, repeating the dangerous cycle.

If you're not eating breakfast, start now. You'll feel hungry later in the morning and that's good. Your body will have been burning energy and fat, and is simply letting you know it's time to replenish. Keep eating good food in moderation throughout the day. Ease off in the evening. Stop eating about three hours before you go to bed. Give it twenty-one days. That's the amount of time required to form a habit. Make it a fundamental part of your life. It's simple and it's effective. Treat the miracle that is your body well. You deserve it.

BREATHE DEEPLY AND STRETCH

Every exercise regimen, every form of yoga, relaxation and meditation incorporates the importance of breathing. Focus on your breathing throughout the day. Breathe deeply. Some programs advocate inhaling and exhaling for equal length duration. Others specify inhaling for a one count, holding for a four count, and exhaling for a two count. I certainly haven't studied every method of breathing, but just breathing comes naturally to us. I've figured out that much. But deep breathing as part of exercise, relaxation and meditation is not necessarily second nature. Find what's most comfortable and natural for you. Find what works for you. Try changing the methods of deep breathing. But be aware of it more.

Think about your breath being drawn in, filling your lungs, and providing the oxygen that fuels your blood stream and your metabolism. Feel its rejuvenating power and energy flow through you. Take time in particular to start and end your day this way. Stretch whenever you can, as much as you can. Let the process limber you up and facilitate the flow of energy through your limbs.

A few years ago, Deb and I were on a soft sand beach at Monkey Mia, a World Heritage Site, on the West Coast of Australia. It was early morning and we hoped to see a pod of wild dolphins come in close to shore, which they do on occasion. Our efforts were rewarded shortly after sunrise when a group of five bottlenose dolphins began to slowly make their way into shallow water. The story goes that about fifty years prior, a local resident befriended and fed the dolphins at that time, and while feeding was no longer allowed, subsequent generations of the dolphins in the area carried on the tradition of loosely interacting with people in the shallows. There was no pattern to the visits.

As the dolphins gradually made their way into shallow water, we noticed a definite formation to their swimming. They were moving in a sort of ring or circle, but still coming towards us, the way a slowly spinning top moves across the ground.

It was then we noticed a tiny, baby dolphin in the middle, and that their circle was obviously protective. By asking around, we figured the baby must have been no more than a couple of weeks old. It was no more than two feet long. The most fascinating thing was that the baby dolphin was still getting used to breathing and co-ordinating swimming at the water's surface. Its breathing was gaspy, like a child who is splashing in deep water for the first time. We were watching the developmental process first hand. It was enchanting. Of course, why would breathing air be a simple, natural thing to a marine mammal? It had to be learned.

We, too, have to learn to breathe in the most effective, relaxing, rejuvenating manner for us as possible. Think about your breathing more. You'll always do it right. Increase your flow of oxygen and increase your energy.

PRAISE YOURSELF

Part of nurturing your highest self and getting in touch with your spirituality is to love and trust yourself. For many of us this is light years away from where we are on life's path. Whether from those around us, our role models, or our culture, we often find it difficult to think highly of ourselves. We forget how magnificent we are, each and every one of us. We are here to live out our divine purpose and we are capable of anything. We embody perfection in our potential. We simply have to remember this. One of the most effective reminders is praise. Praise yourself. The praise must be heartfelt and sincere. Praise freely and praise honestly.

> "BE GOOD TO YOUR BODY.
> WHERE ELSE ARE YOU GOING TO LIVE?"

LOOK LONG AND HARD INTO YOUR EYES
IN A MIRROR AND LOVE WHAT YOU SEE

In nurturing the relationship we have with ourselves, we must come to know who we are. We can look long into the eyes of those we love, and yet we rarely do so with ourselves. Perhaps this is why the relationship we have with ourselves is often weak. We don't give ourselves a chance to look deep within and get to know and love what we see. Love is a choice. We can love whenever we set our minds to it. We can feel love, radiate love and bask in the love we create. Like every choice we make, it begins with you. If you want to change the person you are, then do so. But get to know the person that is you, and get to love who you are.

FORGIVE YOURSELF

Wherever you are right now, whatever emotional baggage you're carrying, let it go. Clean your emotional slate. Give yourself permission to start anew without concern. Learn from what you do. If your actions take you closer to your destination of joy, repeat them, if they do not, do it differently. Continue to seek ways to make things better for yourself.

Visualise yourself writing out the things that you need to forgive yourself for on a blackboard, and consciously, methodically erase them. Brush the chalk dust from the brush and let it all blow away. Learn from it. Do it differently next time. But get on with the here and now, and carry on with certainty towards your goals.

TRUST YOURSELF

Part of recognising that you know what's best is becoming comfortable with who you are. Trusting yourself is the key to strengthening your confidence. Mature the relationship you have with yourself by loving and trusting yourself, and good decisions and a good life will follow. You really do know best. Remember your enthusiasm and your connection with the divine. Perpetuate the positive. Let go, and trust yourself.

When you are faced with decisions, listen carefully to the little voice that helps steer you in the right direction. Forget your past and the roll models that helped establish your current set of beliefs. Deep inside you is the perfect soul that knows best. It will not steer you wrong. All actions occur for a reason, so listen carefully to your inner self. You really do know best.

NO ONE ELSE IS TO BLAME IF YOU'RE UNHAPPY

You are responsible for what you do, what you have, who you are, and how you feel. You are in charge. You control yourself. No one can take that away from you. No one else is to blame if things are not as you'd like them to be. Take a good look in the mirror, remind yourself who's in charge and make what you want for yourself. No one else can.

One of the greatest impediments to achieving what we want is the fact that we don't take responsibility for our actions. We blame others for things that happen to us. We find fault and we feel victimised. You may feel that your set of circumstances puts you at a disadvantage. That's all it is. You feel that way. By changing your feelings and your perception, you change your reality. Treat your life as if it were the most important job you could ever have, for that's what it is. Recognise that you are accountable for this job and you are responsible for the outcome. You're the boss. Big responsibility? You bet. But I wouldn't want it any other way. Take charge and make it right. Change the things you don't like and always look for ways to make things better. Create your happiness. It's all up to you.

DISALLOW BAD MOODS AND BAD HABITS

Our moods and habits will change. Things around us influence us constantly. That's okay. But if a mood or habit is present that you know doesn't coincide with you living the way you want to, disallow it. Like a court reporter striking a comment from the records, have your bad moods and bad habits stricken from your behaviour. Bad moods and bad habits don't make you a bad person. But allowing these things to remain a part of who you are will hold you back. Be aware of it. Take inventory and decide what you want to pack for the journey of your life. Remember you are carrying it all with you. Identify the baggage you no longer want. Throw away the junk that burdens you and slows your progress. Lighten up your pack. You'll literally feel the weight removed, and a spring come back to your step. If I'm taking a flight, I don't want to pay the price for extra baggage. Live life the same way. Travel light, and enjoy the ride.

WE CREATE ALL OF OUR STRESS

As we recognise the fact that we control and design our lives, we must remember that stress, too, is something we create. And if it's in our control, we can change it. If it's not in our control, there's no need for it to concern us.

We create all of our joy and we create all of our stress. Don't let things like the news perpetuate the stress you create. It's just airwaves and ink on paper.

When you feel stress creeping up on you, catch yourself. Recognise what you're feeling. Remind yourself that external events (people and things) can't influence you, only your interpretation of the events can. If you believe that the things that you experience are stressful, then they will be. Your body will respond to your perception accordingly, releasing adrenaline and perpetuating an anxious or stressful physiological state.

Don't believe that things happen to you. Things just happen. It's how you perceive, interpret and respond to things that makes them so. Things don't happen to you. You happen to things. Change your beliefs. Develop a sense of self-reliance. You can interpret events exactly as you choose. When things occur that would traditionally be stressful to you, take a mental step back, remind yourself that you're in charge, and decide how you're going to react to that given event.

Treat challenges as opportunities to solve problems, learn and grow. Think and behave as if you are in absolute control. You soon will be.

"Smokey the Bear" says, "Only you can prevent forest fires." Well, only you can create happiness in your life and only you can create stress in your life too. Dowse the fires of stress. Choose happiness and leave stress behind.

IN THIS MOVIE THAT IS OUR LIFE,
WE ARE NOT ONLY ACTORS, BUT WRITERS,
DIRECTORS AND PRODUCERS.

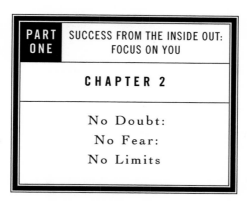

PART ONE — SUCCESS FROM THE INSIDE OUT: FOCUS ON YOU

CHAPTER 2

No Doubt:
No Fear:
No Limits

"*What is genuinely lacking in people is that they do not believe. You are able to obtain in life what your belief will enable you to obtain.*"

— *MOHAMMED ALI*

"*If you knew Who walks beside you on the way that you have chosen, fear would be impossible.*"

— *A COURSE IN MIRACLES*

"*[I]f one advances confidently in the direction of his dreams, and endeavors to live the life which he has imagined, he will meet with a success unexpected in common hours.*"

— *HENRY DAVID THOREAU*

YOU CAN DO EXACTLY AS YOU WISH

If we don't give ourselves permission to passionately pursue greatness and independence, we cannot attain our potential. We are truly capable of anything we set our minds to. We are our only obstacles. Why we forget our pure potential is a result of what we hear from those we are physically and emotionally close to, namely our family and friends. They are our most influential role models. Don't mistake this for blame. It is not. But we develop our personalities and sense of ability from the people closest to us. We buy into the lie that we have limitations. We carry out our parts like actors in a play in which the scene has already been set. But the fact is, in this movie that is our life, we are not only actors, but writers, directors and producers. We can do exactly as we wish. We are born into greatness. It is ours to have. Our potential is limitless.

EVERYTHING THAT MATTERS IS
WITHIN YOUR CONTROL.

YOU HAVE ABSOLUTELY NOTHING TO FEAR

Happiness is a choice. We can choose to be happy or we can choose to be sad. We can choose to love or we can choose the opposite of love, which is fear. Fear is our worst enemy and it is fear, the fear of uncertainty and difference that perpetuates hatred. We create fear and thereby manifest the acts that stem from it. Fear haunts us and keeps us from attaining happiness, success and freedom. Fear holds us back. We fear change. We fear the unknown. The fact is, there's nothing to fear. We must embrace what we don't know, seeking to learn and understand. By embracing change we undermine the very fuel of fear. Once we desire the unknown, seeing it as an opportunity to learn and grow, we no longer have anything to fear. Life becomes a wondrous journey of discovery and joy.

Fear is a false emotion. It's your ego's way of perpetuating the lie that we're separate from the world around us. Think about something that you're afraid of. Spiders? Okay. Think it through to its ultimate conclusion. What are you really afraid of? That spiders would crawl all over you in a swarm, into your ears, nose, mouth and over your eyes, right? You don't know what would happen but you'd lose control and it would feel horrible, wouldn't it? Maybe they'd bite you and you'd die from poison.

Okay, here's the deal. I don't know you or where you live, but I can say with relative certainty that isn't going to happen to you. But the key is to think the fear all the way through to it's conclusion, to eliminate the unknown, thereby changing the irrational into the rational, which can be understood, discounted and eventually eliminated.

Need something bigger? How about the fear of death? That's the big one for most. Let's think it through all the way. You'd be sad because people who love you would miss you. You may feel grief that you will no longer experience this existence. Fair enough. You may regret that you haven't accomplished all that you aspired to (change that now). Are you afraid of being buried or cremated? I can assure you it won't be a concern when the time comes. So what's left? Like all fears it's just a function of not knowing, and feeling a sense of loss (loss of control). When all's said and done, we either have rational fears or irrational fears.

The rational fears we can do something about. (Afraid of hurting yourself or getting sick? Exercise, eat well and be careful). The irrational fears are just that. But by thinking them through to their conclusion, we can bring it back to the concrete and eliminate what underlies all irrational fears and that's the unknown. This is your antidote to all fears. Rational fears can be addressed and eliminated. Irrational fears can be thought through fully and converted into rational fears, which, again, can be addressed and eliminated. Therefore, you have absolutely nothing to fear.

Address your fears. Think them through. If they are rational, change the things that drive the fear. This will negate the fear. If they are irrational, work through them, visualising every option "that could happen". This will bring rationality to the irrational, which enables you to dissolve all fears. Sounds simple, doesn't it? Not necessarily easy, I know, but it is simple. Incorporate support or a coach if need be. There's strength in numbers. But you can certainly do it on your own, successfully, like anything else. Make the choice and know you truly have nothing to fear.

DO WHAT YOU LOVE AND LOVE WHAT YOU DO

Life is precious. Our time is precious, too precious to do anything other than our true calling. We must determine what that calling is and live our lives in harmony with it. Perhaps you already know what it is that you love to do. You just need to make that leap and commit to doing it. If it's your calling, it'll work. Believe in it and believe in yourself. The universe will work out the details, so long as you are true to yourself and do what you love. If you don't love what you do, it's all within your power to change. Make the decision, switch the track your train is running on and change course. Listen to your heart, and do what you love.

GRASP THE CAPABILITIES OF YOUR MIND

Our minds are a direct link to creativity. They represent pure potential, and are the channel through which we turn the metaphysical into the physical, giving substance to the intangible. Think of the mind as a bottomless ocean. Behold its wonder and never forget that we are capable of miracles everyday. It's easy to forget this as we get caught up in a busy life, filled with noise and interference. Catch yourself. Relish that synchronistic event that gave you pause for thought. It's your mind at work, manifesting your thoughts. Knowing this may seem overwhelming, but deep down you know it to be true. What you are truly capable of is beyond your imagination. Dive into your bottomless ocean and grasp the capabilities of your mind.

TAP INTO YOUR CREATIVITY

Many of us fail to ever explore, cultivate and capture our limitless well of creativity. We fall victim to the limits imposed on us by those around us. We believe that the gifts of art, music, poetry and science belong to others, but not us. This is not so. We are all capable of boundless creativity. A few tap into it at levels that amaze us, leaving us to believe that they are gifted while others are not. We think of people like Michelangelo, Mozart and Einstein as people who had something that others don't. The truth is that people like this are blissfully unaware of limitations. Their creativity is pure potential, like drinking from an infinite well. Michelangelo, Mozart and Einstein were only different in that they knew, and never doubted, their potential. They were not afraid to grasp hold of the unmanifest and make it real through art, music and science. Know that you, too, are unbounded potential. Tap into your creativity. Nurture it, enjoy it and practice it.

PUSH YOURSELF

We're capable of such greatness, yet we become complacent in our jobs, our bodies, and our lives. Physical laws apply to us as they do to all bodies of energy. "A body at rest stays at rest, and a body in motion, stays in motion." This doesn't mean we need to be constantly moving to accomplish what we want in our lives. But we limit ourselves to what's easy, rather than pushing ourselves to strive for what we truly want.

This doesn't mean that we should be operating at full speed in order to accomplish our goals. But consistency in our efforts and setting our sights high enables us to move much further in our pursuit of happiness and a fulfilling life.

Running is a good example. A very slow run is actually more difficult than a quick run. The quicker run feels more natural and enables your body to move at a pace for which it was designed. Push your body into a comfortable state of greater motion and you will see how much more you can accomplish.

When Debbie and I were running a marathon in Portland, I began to "hit the wall" around mile twenty-three. We were running together, and with the differences in our strides, I had modified my natural gait to better match Deb's pace. Deb runs quickly, but I have longer legs, so by expending similar amounts of energy, I naturally go slightly faster.

By not running at my natural pace, I was out of synch and feeling the strain on my legs. As we got close to the end of the route, we agreed to run at our own pace. By running at my natural pace, which was faster than I had been running, I reduced the strain on my body. We both finished the race feeling significantly better than we had three miles prior.

I also experience the benefit of pushing myself at work. I don't believe that hard work is required to succeed. But we do have a natural pace that's often greater than our usual working pace. I consistently find that when I'm focussing on a lot of things in my workday, I accomplish an enormous amount efficiently and effectively. However, if I have only one or two menial things to do, they tend to take a long time to complete and I often find myself making mistakes or doing a poor job.

Find your natural pace. I suspect you're capable of moving faster and getting more done with greater ease. The process can be fun and empowering.

ONLY YOU CAN HOLD YOURSELF BACK

You are responsible for everything in your life. No one else is. People may compliment you and praise you, but only you can decide whether or not to feel good about yourself. By the same token, no one else is able to limit you in your endeavours. Recognize your boundlessness. Only you can hold yourself back. Catch yourself if you find yourself doubting or thinking about reasons why something seems impossible. Start over again, knowing that you're not being completely honest. Don't let the walls of doubt build up. Break them down, and do whatever you want with an open, unlimited mind.

YOU ARE WORTHY

Know your enemy. Sherlock Holmes had Professor Moriarty. Superman had Lex Luthor. For us, it's our ego. Our egos fuel our fears and doubts and undermine our natural ability to rise up and perpetuate joy. In *The Art of War*, Sun Tzu explains that the ultimate victory is to outwit your opponent and therefore triumph without engaging the enemy. This is how we can defeat our egos. We can win without ever having to confront our adversary. Start by knowing that you are worthy of anything and everything you desire. Program this knowledge into all of your thoughts and actions. When ego tries to undermine you or blindside you with uncertainty, defend yourself by side-stepping the onslaught, like an elegant bullfighter in the Basque tradition. Victory is not in the death of the opponent, but in the successful outmanoeuvring of the opponent. Let your opponent's energy expend itself, bypassing you completely. Focus on the next positive thing you choose to bring into your life. You needn't empower your ego. You're above it all in your pursuit of happiness.

ELIMINATE EXPECTATIONS

Expectations require judgement. And judgement separates us from others. Judgement fuels the notion of right and wrong, good and bad. And while we live in a world of duality, it is not real. Judgement perpetuates fear and disappointment, and judgement underlies all expectations. If you have expectations of your loved ones, family, friends or co-workers, you are imposing rules on these people, and your ego has appointed you judge and jury. This leads to disappointment and drives a wedge into the relationships that we should nurture and treasure. Eliminating expectations removes that wedge and strengthens these relationships.

By eliminating expectations, we forgo judgement. Release it. Let it go. Judgement is a weight we carry with us and it perpetuates the lie that we are different. It is ego rearing its ugly head again, deceiving us into believing that we are separate from those around us. Don't buy into the lie. Release judgement.

THINGS DON'T HAPPEN *TO YOU*. *YOU* HAPPEN *TO* THINGS.

SHRINK YOUR EGO

Your ego is your one true enemy. It is what fuels envy, dissatisfaction and fear. It is the devil that whispers in one ear when you are faced with difficult decisions and it is the voice that offers up the weak choice, a seemingly easier choice, but inevitably the wrong choice. On a physical level, the ego can contribute to material gain such as a well-paying job, a big house, a fancy car, promotions and recognition. Your ego drives you to attain and to have more than others, climbing a traditional "ladder of success". But these accomplishments will ultimately be hollow if ego is all that is driving you, for the ego is insatiable. Whatever you attain, it will never be enough for your ego. There will always be someone else that your ego wants you to surpass.

The ego is a parasite, and will gnaw away at the real you, leaving you emotionally hungry and dissatisfied. For this reason we must shrink the ego, and nurture the angel's voice that also whispers to us when we make every decision in our lives. That voice may not lead us to the easiest choice, but it will always be the best choice.

RELINQUISH NEGATIVITY

Negative energy will always exist. It's part of the grand equilibrium with positive energy. Both types of energy will always bombard you. But like everything in our lives, you have the ability to choose. You can choose what you absorb and what you deflect. Soak up positive energy and send it out stronger. Do not take ownership of negative energies such as stress, fear, doubt and anger.

Negativity, like a positive mental attitude, is habitual. It's addictive, and breaking that addiction can be as challenging as breaking an addiction to any substance. But it must be broken if we are to attain happiness in our lives. Unfortunately, we don't have many programs, clinics or patches to break the habit of negativity. I've yet to hear of a family intervention to quash a loved one's negativity. But fortunately, the antidote to negativity lies within us in abundance. In the same way that light destroys dark, positive energy and love will overpower negative energy and fear. Let the light in and relinquish negativity.

EMBRACE YOUR POSITIVE ENERGY

Part of relinquishing negativity is nurturing and building up our positive energy flow. You can focus your attention on your positive energy and it will take care of the negative for you. It has no choice, like water flowing downhill and filling the space it runs to, positive energy will fill the vacuum that negativity creates. The key is for us to be aware of the powerful positive energy that is around us that we can tap into and add to. As you heighten your awareness of your positive energy, feel yourself immersed in it like a luxurious hot pool. But know that the source of that warmth and that comfort is you. And know that the level of that container of goodness is also determined by you. Keep filling it until it overflows and radiates out, washing over the space around you, wherever you are.

> IF YOU CAN CONTROL OR INFLUENCE
> SOMETHING TO CHANGE IT FOR THE BETTER,
> DO SO. IF NOT, LET IT GO.

DO SOMETHING YOU'VE NEVER DONE BEFORE

What makes children laugh when they play? They experience pure joy in their sense of discovery. They are human sponges, soaking up the world around them as they learn. It's all new and it's wondrous. As we age we tend to lose this wonderful sense of learning and exploration. But we can recapture it easily. Let yourself see the world as a child does. See things with a renewed spirit. Make it fresh. Feel wonder and do something that you have never done before. It doesn't have to be skydiving, but it may be. It may be swimming in the ocean, or tasting a food that is new to you. It may be that you are completely open and honest with someone, letting them know that you care about them very much. It may be picking up a new book, or sitting outside, enjoying a different view. But do it today. Repeat this type of behaviour regularly and you will again have the world anew for you. Let the child within go out and play.

> NOBODY CAN TRULY INFLUENCE
> YOU WITHOUT YOUR PERMISSION.

PART ONE	SUCCESS FROM THE INSIDE OUT: FOCUS ON YOU

CHAPTER 3

Having All
That You Want

"Happiness and love are just a choice away."

— *LEO BUSCAGLIA*

"Whatever you vividly imagine, ardently desire, sincerely believe, and enthusiastically act upon will inevitably come to pass."

— *PAUL J. MEYER*

"The expression of gratitude is a powerful force that generates even more of what we have already received."

— *DEEPAK CHOPRA*

BE YOURSELF

You can be exactly as you wish to be. Break the shackles you wear as the result of your upbringing. Be independent of the good opinion of others. Hear the rhythm that's inside of you and dance to the beat. It's not always easy. There's risk involved. Your ego will fight you, sending out messages of embarrassment, self consciousness, fear and doubt. Turn down the volume on that noise and turn up your inner drummer. Let it beat loud and true. Believe in you. Fear nothing. Be as you wish to be and be who you truly are.

EXPRESS YOURSELF

Trust in what you think. Believe in how you feel. What you want to do and say is important. Do not worry about the fear and doubt that holds you back. Embarrassment is only your ego in disguise. What your ego tells you is unimportant. Ignore the little devil on your shoulder. Maybe people won't respond in the manner you'd like. It doesn't matter. Feel the joy in who you are and express yourself.

MAKE A COMMITMENT TO YOURSELF
AND DO NOT WAVER FROM IT

We are designed for accomplishment. Few of us ever test the boundaries of what we're capable of. Achievement is our very nature. It is divine. Know what you want. Stretch yourself. Decide, then make a commitment to yourself and do not waver from it.

It may be a change in your job, improving a relationship, having a richer life, being healthier or learning a new skill. Only you know what you truly want. Maybe you haven't yet given yourself permission to visualise it. Do so now. Keep doing it. All reality stems from thought, good and bad. You can design the life you want and live it fully. Once you've given yourself permission to identify what it is you want, continually focus on that and reinforce it into physical reality. Do not waiver from what you want. You are worth it and you deserve it. Be true to yourself.

EVERYTHING THAT MATTERS IS WITHIN YOUR CONTROL

Everything that matters is within your control. This should be read again, slowly. If something isn't within your control, it shouldn't matter to you. It may interest you, but it can't be a cause of concern, worry or stress. Either you can influence it, and therefore change it for the better, or you can't, so it should no longer concern you. For example, if you read or watch the news, you'll likely feel for those who suffer. This is natural. After all, people in the news are part of the same grand dance as you and me. But there's no need to worry about anything that you can't control. The best examples I can think of are weather, traffic and the stock market. We worry far too much over what we can't control. Let these worries go. Free up the space in your mind for joy or silence.

You're mistaken if you believe things just happen to you for no reason at all. The universe is playing its one song with perfect harmony. We're all a part of the orchestration, each with our pivotal part to play. We are not merely actors. We direct and produce the lives we live. All that will happen to us remains not only in our control, but also entirely within our design.

STRIVE TO UNDERSTAND

Strive to understand people's beliefs, behaviour, cultures, religion and rituals. Let judgement fade away. Become a pupil. Learn and grow. So many of our problems stem from our unwillingness to work at understanding. A lack of understanding fosters fear, and fear makes differences appear where there really are none. By striving to understand, we break down the false walls of difference and eliminate fear.

RECOGNISE YOUR WEALTH

We are wealthy. Every single one of us. Whether it's wealth in love, health, comfort or opportunity, we are all wealthy. We forget that when our egos compare ourselves with others. Our egos judge and focus on differences in material things, such as money, cars, homes or titles on a business card. These are only labels, and labels are a means of differentiation. We are not different. We're not different from someone who's homeless nor are we different from someone who's a billionaire. We've simply made different choices throughout our lives. Some people seem to have been born into greater opportunity. But those who succeed are brought up with greater expectations and a greater awareness of opportunity. We can model the behaviour of anyone we choose and be as happy, healthy and successful as we desire. Whatever we wish is ours for the making and we can start immediately by recognising our wealth.

LIVE WITHIN YOUR MEANS
AND BEYOND YOUR EXPECTATIONS

We can have immeasurably rich lives by enjoying what we have. Things don't have to have a dollar value to be valuable. Know what you earn and enjoy it, make the most of it, put a little away and give some away every time you get some. It will perpetuate abundance for you. The same goes for everything else in your life. Love, joy and kindness perpetuate themselves. They are limitless in quantity. So is money. Watch your expenses, but remember to live richly and know that your expectations should be limitless. The well of wealth can never be exhausted.

SIT SILENTLY FOR ONE MINUTE

Silence is the space between noises. It is said that it is the silence between notes that makes music. Silence represents rest, rejuvenation, meditation and prayer. It is where creation happens. Silence is the environment where we can manifest and make our dreams real. Sit silently for one minute. Clear your mind. Do it again. Your mind will likely be filled with chatter and noise. Turn down the volume on that inner voice. It's just your ego staying busy and fighting for survival. Silence diminishes your ego. Silence fuels you with creativity and positive power. Jump into it and embrace silence.

GO BEYOND WISHING AND HOPING
AND DECIDE. DECISIVELY DETERMINE WHAT
YOU WANT WITH CLARITY.

BE AWARE OF YOUR SPIRITUALITY

Repetition is the mother of skill, and skill is the mother of mastery. Life coach and motivational guru Tony Robbins emphasises this principal throughout his great books and lectures. To attain a level of mastery in our lives, we must program ourselves for success. Remind yourself again and again of your potential and of your worthiness. Tap into it and become aware of your spirituality.

We are truly spiritual beings here in human form. From the moment of our conception, our lives are creative miracles. As we grow we forget about our connection with the divine. But we can recapture it. For some it strikes like a lightening bolt, for others it's a lifelong process. But it's there for us to tap into whenever we make the choice. All it takes is a decision, belief, and remembering.

WHATEVER YOU ATTAIN, IT WILL
NEVER BE ENOUGH FOR YOUR EGO.

LIVE NOW

Eckert Tolle captured the peace and potential of the present with beautiful clarity in his book *The Power of Now*. After all, now is all we have. Our lives become richer when we live in the present moment. This mind-set is a powerful catalyst to keep negativity at bay. All of our stresses are time-based. We feel guilt for things that have happened and we worry about what may come to pass. Living in the immediate present dissolves the useless emotions of guilt and worry. Live freely. Live richly. Live now.

IT'S OKAY TO WANT, BUT DO SOMETHING ABOUT IT

We are designed to achieve. Wants and needs drive our desire to achieve and acquire. This doesn't have to mean material things. But it may. At our most basic level we need food and water for survival and then we require safety. In terms of rudimentary survival, this may mean the decision of "fight or flight". In one of his audio programs, Deepak Chopra refers, tongue in cheek, to the "Four F's" essential to the survival of the species: feeding, fighting, fleeing and, of course, procreation.

But as we expand our model of needs and wants, so too do we increase our desires. It may be greater physical comfort, greater joy or heightened peace of mind. This is natural and positive. Our minds want to create. A painter wants and needs to paint. A writer wants and needs to write. Children want and need to play, imagine and discover. Our minds are driven in the same way. They are perfectly designed to think and to create. Don't deny your mind's purpose. It's your fundamental and definitive purpose to want and to achieve. It's perfectly natural to want, but it's not okay to not do anything about it. Act on your desire. Make your dreams your reality.

SEE, FEEL AND KNOW
YOUR SUCCESS AND YOUR HAPPINESS

Wayne Dyer is a wonderful author and speaker. He has been instrumental in enabling many of us to live richer and more joyful lives. His book, *You'll See It When You Believe It,* captures the essence of these words. Like an athlete that visualises herself winning a race and standing on the podium, we can visualise and manifest whatever we want. We think things into being. We create our reality by what we see in our mind's eye. See what you want to see. See your success and your happiness. Feel it. Know it. Live it. Let every fibre of your being reinforce it. Then enjoy it.

SILENCE ENABLES US TO GET INTO
THE CREATIVE GAP AND MANIFEST ALL THAT
WE WISH TO BE AND HAVE.

KNOW THAT YOU ARE...

Knowing is our highest level of understanding. We can hope. We can have faith. We can believe. Or we can know. Knowing denotes absolute certainty. The following is a list of concepts to know if we are to be happy, live joyfully, and to be at peace. This list is not intended to be exhaustive, but each point is extremely powerful and reinforces what we know to be true at our highest level. Like any prayer or credo, these thoughts or affirmations should not be rushed. Think about each statement slowly, carefully, and methodically. Let it become a part of who you are. Then it will become real and you will know it to be true.

NO ONE ELSE IS TO BLAME IF THINGS ARE
NOT AS YOU'D LIKE THEM TO BE.

Know that you are loved.
Know that you are special.
Know that you are beautiful.
Know that you are spiritual.
Know that you love.
Know that you control your destiny.
Know that you determine your fate.
Know that you are capable of wondrous things.
Know that you can accomplish anything you desire.
Know that you can accomplish everything
you set your mind to do.
Know that you and God are one.
Know that you are not alone.
Know that you are limitless.
Know that you are eternal.

YOU DESERVE IT ALL

The world will change for the better if we embrace the words of Marianne Williamson, made famous by Nelson Mandela.

"Our deepest fear is not that we are inadequate.
Our deepest fear is that we are powerful beyond
measure. It is our light, not our darkness that
frightens us. We ask ourselves, who am I to be
brilliant, gorgeous, talented, fabulous?

Actually, who are we not to be?

You are a child of God. Your playing small doesn't
serve the world. There's nothing enlightened about
shrinking so that other people won't feel insecure
around you. We were born to make manifest the
glory of God that is within us. It's not just in some of
us, it's in everyone. And as we let our light shine, we
unconsciously give others permission to do the same.

As we are liberated from our own fears,
our presence automatically liberates others."

Know that you are worthy of everything. Remember it always. Create for yourself everything you want.

AFFIRMATION QUESTION

What's the nicest
thing that's happened
to you today?

APPLICATION EXERCISE
— FOR YOUR MIND —

What's one thing
that you can do,
right now, to improve
yourself mentally?

Write it down as a
goal for yourself. Set
a deadline for doing it.
Commit to doing it.

Remind yourself that you are wonderful. This isn't about pumping yourself up with flattery. This is about getting in the habit of not beating up on yourself, and replacing that negativity with regular, positive self-praise. It's not that you're better than others; it's that you are becoming a better person than you were yesterday. Remember that everyone came from somewhere. One of my best friends went from being bankrupt, divorced, and overweight to running a marathon, having a wonderful marriage and family and becoming a self-made millionaire. Shania Twain and Oprah Winfrey are wonderful examples of people who endured hardship and through drive, hard work and giving of themselves, have made phenomenally successful lives for themselves and those they love. Nelson Mandela is another inspirational example, having transcended from prison to presidency.

But it doesn't have to be about coming from poverty, enduring hardship and turning yourself into a multi-millionaire. Another friend of mine whom I work with is someone that I consider to be fabulously successful. She got out of an abusive marriage and single-handedly did a great job of raising her two daughters, working hard and making a great career for herself. She's now happily engaged to a great guy who loves her and her daughters — all because she never lost sight of her potential. And while it was tough most days, she taught her girls to be positive, happy, and helpful and to have a great work ethic. That shows remarkable success and accomplishment.

My point is that we must realise that we are capable of greatness. Identify a successful person that inspires you and work to adopt the traits that made them successful. Think of that person as your mentor or role model. It could be someone you've read about or it could be a friend or a family member. It could be an historical figure or even a fictional character. It may be that single mom who balances parenting with a career. It could be someone who has overcome addiction or beaten cancer. Or it could be the person who lead a successful life and made it better through dedicated giving and charity.

Find the person you want to emulate. Live your life in accordance with what you want to become. Start with a daily activity, such as taking a course. It could be at a technical school or an art class or it could be learning a musical instrument. You might have to sacrifice something else in order to afford the time or the tuition. That represents discipline and commitment. Think big scale, and then implement small scale. Baby steps can take you to the highest peak. Focus on your ultimate goal, and then take consistent action to get there. No one simply summits Mount Everest. It's about planning, getting help, getting fit, and starting out. You'll experience set-backs and your determination can be tested every day. Don't let set-backs keep you from progressing. Rest, recuperate, and then keep going. Most parties that summit Mount Everest, for example, aren't successful the first time. But those who succeed do not give up.

Feed your mind with positive thoughts. Start the day by telling yourself, with genuine conviction, that you're great and you can do anything. You can accomplish anything that comes your way at work; you can handle any family crisis and you can, today, take positive action that will move you closer to your goals.

Get a positive book and read it. The self-help section of most book stores is continuously growing. Your mind will love the break from television and you'll feel great about taking this exceptional step towards improving your life. If you don't want to buy a book in case you might not like it, go to the library. And many great titles are available on CD if that fits your schedule better. Some of my favourite inspirational authors, who have helped me to consistently improve myself and live a better life, are Wayne Dyer, Tony Robbins, Phil McGraw, Deepak Chopra, Robin Sharma, Elaine St. James, Marianne Williamson, Jack Canfield, Dale Carnegie, Napoleon Hill, Zig Ziglar, Richard Carlson, Robert Fulghum, Brock Tully, David Irvine, Eckhart Tolle, James Redfield, Dan Millman, Larry Winget, Mark Victor Hansen and Neale Donald Walsch.

If you're serious about improving your life, then commit to it. Most people who start reading a book do not finish it, let alone implement something positive from it. Don't be like my overweight friend who jokes that dieting obviously works for him, as he's lost thousands of pounds over the course of his life. And we all know someone who has quit smoking dozens of times. It's the same thing as when I go to the gym and it's always packed in early January following the New Year's resolutions, but inevitably it's quiet again by the end of the month. I can't help but think that a lot of people pay a lot of money for those two-week gym memberships. Don't let that be you!

APPLICATION EXERCISE
— FOR YOUR BODY —

What's one thing
that you can do,
right now, to improve
yourself physically?

Write it down as a
goal for yourself. Set
a deadline for doing it.
Commit to doing it.

Take better care of your body. Try a new or additional exercise. Start your day with some stretching and deep breathing. There are a plethora of books and programs on fitness, exercise and diet. Try one out and see if you like it. Remember it takes three full weeks of consistent action to form a new habit. Don't fall into the procrastination trap. Act now, right now.

One of my friends will discretely do a few sit-up crunches regularly, throughout the day. We may be sitting outside or watching TV. He doesn't make a show of it; he's simply comfortable in his environment. He behaves in the same way whether he's alone or with close friends. I admire his centeredness and quiet confidence. And he's in better shape than anyone I know.

Try doing one, two, or three dozen crunches or sit-ups to start your day. If it's tough, start with fewer. If it's easy, do a few more. You will see a significant increase in your physical and mental energy. Not only will you benefit physiologically, but you'll feel a great mental charge as you consciously take control of yourself and how you live.

Set the alarm 30 minutes earlier in the morning, and go for a 15-20 minute walk to start your day and finish with a piece or two of fresh fruit, some juice, and some water. You'll have more energy as a result and your body will burn extra calories. Do it for yourself but trust me, those around you will notice your increased energy. Your enthusiasm will almost certainly increase as a result of the positive hormones generated by exercise and diet, such as noradrenalin, endorphins and serotonins, which will fuel better moods for longer periods of time. This can make you feel better at work and provide you with the energy and focus to pursue additional activities that are important to you outside of work, and that's what will enable you to live a fuller, richer more satisfying life than most.

I wanted to lose ten pounds after a wonderful month in Australia, where I had indulged regularly on fish and chips and beer. This is how I went about it.

I wrote down my goal. With all due respect to the diet and weight-loss gurus, I like to keep things as simple as possible, so I came up with my own "Three Way" fitness program:

1. Eat *way* less.
2. Eat *way* healthier.
3. Exercise *way* more.

My program may seem vague and simplistic but it made perfect sense to me and as a result it worked for me. The implementation required conscious choices consistently. If it was "time to eat", I'd ask myself if I was actually hungry, or if I was simply reacting from habit, that is, I always eat at this time. So I began to eat a little less frequently. But when I was hungry, I would consciously eat a smaller portion than I was used to. This method of food intake has been proven successful with a number of diet plans that monitor the quantity of food you eat. I would also drink an extra glass of water, which is good in and of itself, and it made me feel full. When I ate, I would make a conscious choice to prepare something rather than getting fast food take-out. I would minimize the intake of fatty foods and eat more fresh, natural foods. And with respect to exercise, while I was used to running for about 20-25 minutes most days, I increased this to about 40-45 minutes. I found this simple but effective. I lost the weight I intended to in a month, all because of writing out my goal and then taking consistent action and making conscious choices that took me closer to my goal, until I ultimately reached it. You can do the same. It starts with baby steps, but commitment and consistency are critical to accomplish what's important to you.

APPLICATION EXERCISE
— FOR YOUR SPIRIT —

What's one thing
that you can do,
right now, to improve
yourself spiritually?

Write it down as a
goal for yourself. Set
a deadline for doing it.
Commit to doing it.

Irrespective of religious beliefs (or lack thereof) there is wonderful, life-affirming power in giving thanks. You don't even have to "give thanks" to anyone or anything. Simply be thankful. Appreciate and be grateful for the things you have and plan to have. This is something I initially learned from self-help and spiritual readings. Give thanks for what you want to come to pass, that is, for what you want to have in your life. Feel gratitude as though what you want is already in your possession and you are experiencing it in your life now.

Deb and I took a personal financial risk a number of years ago. We purchased a beautiful cottage. We stretched ourselves financially at the time, going heavily into debt to acquire it, but we loved the place. It became our special sanctuary and we had many beautiful experiences there with family, friends and nature. And every time we were there, I would not allow thoughts of financial anxiety to pervade my thinking. At night I would stand alone on the wooden deck, looking out into the dark of the Ponderosa pines and up to the stars, which were brilliant as we were far from city lights. I would smell the richness of the trees and hear frogs croaking and the occasional hoot of an owl or howl of a coyote. And I gave thanks, every night, for having earned the income to pay off the debt and make the cottage ours. For two years that was not the reality of the situation, but I continued to be grateful for having accomplished the financial goal all the same. And during the week I would go back to work, writing down goals, working hard with conviction, commitment and unwavering certainty that the money would come and the debt would be paid and the cottage would be ours. I do not believe I did anything different at work, where a large portion of my income is commission and therefore in my control. The only significant difference was my written goal of earning the income and my consistently giving thanks for having already accomplished the goal. And a little over two years later, not only was the debt paid, but we had made a handsome gain on the value of the cottage as well. Yes, I worked hard, but I believe that by emoting gratitude with the conviction of success I realised my goal much faster than by simply behaving like an ostrich and hoping it would all be okay somehow, or never having taken the risk in the first place. I felt responsible for manifesting the successful attainment of my goal and thereby being able to create great memories for Deb and me and our family and friends at this special place.

When setting a goal for yourself, plan big and implement small. Question: How do you eat an elephant? Answer: One bite at a time.

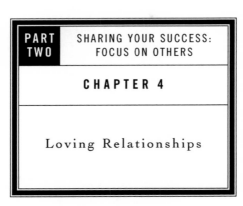

PART
TWO

SHARING YOUR SUCCESS:
FOCUS ON OTHERS

CHAPTER 4

Loving Relationships

"When you have the choice between being right and kind, always choose kind."

— *WAYNE DYER*

"We attract to us what we first become."

— *LARRY WINGET*

"Whatever you want, wants you."

— *MARK VICTOR HANSEN*

LOVE PROACTIVELY

Love isn't something that happens to you. You don't just fall into love, despite what we may enjoy watching in the movies. Love is something that comes from within. We create it and foster it, allowing it to bubble up within us and blossom. From within, it radiates out. Like everything that we experience, we create it for ourselves. Feel love. Make love. Send love. Don't look for it, create it. Treat love as it is, a perfect action.

Love is something that we must first do. We experience it, we feel it and then we give it away. Love is an action. Love freely and fully. Love as if you're in charge of gift giving, and love is all you have, and you have an endless supply of it. It fits everyone perfectly.

FEEL LOVE EVERY DAY

When we are aware of something, we can embrace it and enjoy its presence in our lives. Love is something we usually take for granted or we want more. Become aware of the love in your life. It may be a relationship, the world around you or part of who you are, but get to know it. Love is there to be enjoyed and shared. The more you're aware of it, the more you can enjoy it and its momentum will grow. Love's momentous power is like an all-season snowball of purity and light that keeps getting bigger and brighter. It's there for all of us. Feel it at all times throughout every day.

TELL THAT PERSON YOU LOVE THEM

Don't keep your love a secret. Maybe it's even a secret to you. Be generous. It doesn't have to be an event or have a whole lot of hoopla around it. It doesn't have to be that frequent. But it does have to be consistent and sincere. Think about your feelings. Is it in you? I can assure you it is. Get in touch with it. There is nothing better. It means opening yourself up and that can be scary, but the greater the risk, the greater the reward. Don't be afraid. Open up to the power of love. Tell that person you love them.

LOVE IS A CHOICE.

CALL THAT PERSON YOU'VE BEEN MEANING TO CALL

Have you ever been thinking of someone and that person calls you on the phone? We've all had wonderful glimpses of that synchronicity. Never discount it. Coincidence doesn't mean random chance; it is the coinciding of events perfectly and it happens on purpose. Be aware of it. We can be tuned in to the world around us much more than we know.

Maybe you've been thinking of someone but haven't yet called them. Maybe you just haven't made the time, or perhaps the call is a difficult one to make. That person, very likely, feels the same way. The fact that you've had the thought but not acted on it is detrimental to you and the person you thought about.

Be good to yourself and to someone else. Make the time and call someone you've been meaning to call. Don't wait. Live your life as if it's finite and know that it's not. Say what you feel. Treasure relationships. Make a quick call. Maybe it's a friend or a relative. Just touch base. You may share something kind, funny or uplifting with them or you may be providing an outlet for them to share with you. Remember, no conditions or expectations. Just call.

CALL PEOPLE ON THEIR BIRTHDAYS

Making friends and making people feel good is surprisingly easy. Call people on their birthdays. Even if they say they don't like to acknowledge another birthday, they'll feel good to know someone has thought of them and someone cares. Birthdays, like names, are something we hold dear. We see these things as an integral part of who we are. Acknowledging a birthday reinforces your acknowledgement of that person. It's not about who called who last or even if they called. Call. It's thoughtful, it's kind and it's positive.

WRITE A KIND NOTE TO SOMEONE

Visits are special. Phone calls are great. But letters and notes share a different level of intimacy between writer and recipient. We often write with greater candour than we speak. Writing not only shows a commitment of time and effort, but we usually capture the sentiment of important thoughts or feelings better through the written word. We often write with greater clarity, unafraid to be poetic or vivid in descriptions.

Deb and I received a great postcard from our relatives when they were travelling in Southeast Asia. On the postcard they drew a simple map of the area they'd trekked through and added a drawing of a monkey to show where they'd had their first sighting. It was a simple cartoon-style sketch, but it made the communication fun and graphic. In reading the note and enjoying the drawing, we were right there, with them, sharing their adventure.

Writing is the most effective way of sharing from the heart. It doesn't have to be a lengthy letter. It'll always be special and well received when written with sincerity.

> WITHOUT TOTAL FORGIVENESS,
> WE WILL ALWAYS CARRY THE WEIGHT
> OF RESENTMENT OR REMORSE.

LIKE PEOPLE

Some people may not strike you as likeable. I understand. It may be tough to do, but do your best. Look hard for something likeable in everyone.

No matter how it may seem at times, we're all pretty much the same. We're all identical at the subatomic level and we're all on the same journey. We just appear different at different times and given different circumstances. We adopt different opinions, cultures and beliefs. But we can see through the entire jumble if we choose to. We can get rid of the lenses that distort our perception of others and ourselves. There's good in all of us. There's something to be liked in everyone. We just need to see it. It's worth it for all of us. Work at liking everyone.

ASK WHAT PEOPLE DO

Ask questions. That's how we learn, and that's how we grow. But we become enraptured with the sound of our own voice and we get comfortable with our own thoughts and opinions. Get off the selfish treadmill. Start asking people about themselves. Find out who they really are.

Take the emphasis off "me" and draw others into your world. Broaden your interest.

Start by learning what people do. We often associate our jobs with who we are. It's an easy trap to fall into. Work gets the greatest amount of our attention during the day. You may say, "I'm a banker", "I'm a clerk", or "I'm an architect", but that can't be who you really are. These work-related labels aren't accurate, but they're a good starting point to get to know people. Don't think about what you're going to say next. Just let people talk about what they do. Open the lines of communication.

REMEMBER PEOPLE'S NAMES

"What's in a name?" I heard a comedian say, "If you broke wind, and it wasn't called a fart, would it still smell bad?" Ah, philosophy. I'm not willing to tackle that one, but I know the importance of names. Our names are our labels. If someone asks you, "Who are you?" you will respond by giving your name. People's names are extremely important. Many of us don't try hard enough with people's names, whether we are pronouncing them correctly or whether we're just remembering them. Try harder. Learn to pronounce people's names and remember people's names. Anything less takes away from them and from you.

MAKE FRIENDS

It's been said that if you have one good friend, you're wealthy. I don't believe you need even one friend to be wealthy, but I believe one friend does increase your wealth. I also believe that more good friends increase your wealth exponentially and we should constantly be increasing our wealth. Friendship can be easy and it can also take effort. Know that it's always worth it, whatever your friendship may go through. Work at increasing your wealth. Open up your mind. Open up yourself. We do it naturally when we are kids. Regain that openness and regain the pleasure of being child-like. Make a new friend.

SINCERELY COMPLIMENT SOMEONE YOU JUST MET

Look for ways to be kind. Compliment. Do it sincerely and do it frequently. Believe what you say and say what you feel. Strengthen the positive and reinforce the good. Sincerely compliment someone, then go one step further and sincerely compliment someone you just met.

TALK DOWN TO NO ONE

Relinquish judgement. Catch yourself if you start to feel judgemental. There's no need to feel guilty or envious of anyone. We're all in this together. Think highly of people and you help make it so. We're all doing our thing together, after all. See people for who they aspire to be. See people for their potential and capabilities. Treat people with the dignity, kindness and love that you feel you deserve. Talk down to no one.

Remember we're really all the same. We appear different sometimes, but that's just perception. Broaden your circle of influence. Connect with more people. There's strength in unity. Look for the positive in everyone and find that connection.

BE KIND

It is not always easy. Sometimes it's downright difficult. But usually it's the most natural thing in the world. All living things need warmth and kindness, whether it's a plant reaching towards the light, a pet wanting to be cuddled, or people wanting to be hugged and loved. By giving warmth and kindness, you always get more back. Make the effort.

Give people credit for what they do and what they try to do. Give people credit for who they are. Think about why people behave the way they do. Have patience. Be kind. Everyone benefits.

LOVE IS SOMETHING THAT WE MUST FIRST DO.
LOVE IS AN ACTION.

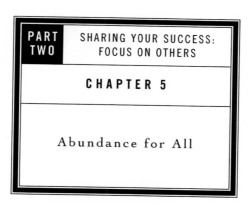

PART TWO — SHARING YOUR SUCCESS: FOCUS ON OTHERS

CHAPTER 5

Abundance for All

"The secret of prosperity is generosity, for by sharing with others the good that life gives us we open up the well springs of abundance."

— J. DONALD WALTERS

"Helping others make money and helping other people to fulfill their desires is a sure way to ensure you'll make money for yourself as well as more easily fulfill your own dreams."

— DEEPAK CHOPRA

"If we do what we love, love what we do, and express ourselves fully and freely, we are serving others in accordance to our purpose. All that is left is for us to open ourselves to receive."

— ARNOLD PATENT

HELP THAT PERSON WHO NEEDS IT

We all know someone who could use a little help. It may be as simple as a bit of companionship. It may be financial. It may be help with a particular task, something they want to accomplish. They very likely won't ask for your help. But they might. It feels good to be needed. It's good to know you have a friend and that you are a friend. Don't ignore it. Respond. Help that person who you know could use it.

VISIT WITH A HOMELESS PERSON

We all have different challenges. Some are overwhelming, some are non-existent, but we're all in the same boat. We may begin our lives from different starting lines, but we all had a starting line. Never forget how fortunate you are. Give thanks. Help as much as you can. Never judge. Visiting with a homeless person can make an enormous difference. You'll provide a bit of friendship to someone who could probably use it. Your perception will change. You'll very likely learn something.

Over the course of about a year, I came to know a homeless man who lived in our neighbourhood. We would often sit together on a bench and visit. We came to know quite a lot of each other through our conversations. For a number of years he had worked in a research capacity at one of the local universities. He had a gifted mind, but he was often medicated due to a psychological imbalance and as a result, he had great difficulty coping with the day-to-day routine of a traditional, demanding work environment. The stress that he felt as a result of his condition and his life was too much for him. He left his job, and without income or family, was soon on the street. He had been homeless for over ten years. He said he missed some elements of his old life, but for the most part he felt his choices were right for him. He did not feel that he was lacking. He never asked me for money.

> GRATITUDE PERPETUATES ABUNDANCE.

STOP AND LISTEN TO A STREET BUSKER

There are all kinds of street buskers: musicians, jugglers and entertainers. You may consider some extremely talented, while others may not appeal to your tastes. You may feel accosted, annoyed or even guilty just by their presence. But know that whatever their story, it takes an enormous amount of courage and confidence to do what they're doing.

I took the time to sit and listen to a soft-spoken young man who was playing a song he had written on his very beaten up acoustic guitar. I believe it was the only song he had written and he was visibly delighted that someone cared to hear it. He sang it with passion and it was really quite lovely. By doing this, he was completely opening up his soul, and we were immediately connected. You may say "good for you" to me, but I say "good for him". Very few people have the courage to open themselves up that way to someone they've just met. We were both immeasurably richer as a result of it. All because I stopped and really listened.

GIVE THAT PERSON SOME MONEY

Give a little money to someone you see on the street. Don't think too much about it and don't make a big deal out of it. Give a little and give thanks for the fact that you have it to give away. Don't judge and don't have any expectations. Just give a bit. Feel sincerely good about it. The universe will replenish it (with interest) once you don't expect it.

WHEN TIPPING, ASK YOURSELF, "WHO NEEDS IT MORE?"

When tipping, round up. No matter how bad your day may have been, you still have someone serving you. They're at work and you're not. Cut your server some slack. Be kind. Use first names when it feels appropriate. And when tipping, practice the rules of generosity and abundance; give a little more. It'll mean much more to the recipient and it'll do a lot more for you.

PAY FOR THE COFFEE OF THE PERSON BEHIND YOU IN LINE

Random acts of kindness are changing the world. Stories of kindness lift us up and inspire us. But don't just enjoy the stories. Become one. Do something thoughtful and generous. It can be relatively simple, but it perpetuates joy, goodness and love. It's difficult for someone to be negative when they're inundated with kindness.

Pay for the coffee of the person behind you in line. Don't wait for their thanks. You will need to round up when paying and that means a nice tip for the server. Think of it as a bonus act of kindness, like a two-for-one. It'll require a surprising amount of courage and confidence to do it and you'll be opening yourself up to a great deal of uncertainty. That's good. Do it anyway. It may not change the world, but I believe it will.

COINCIDENCE DOESN'T MEAN RANDOM CHANCE; IT IS THE COINCIDING OF EVENTS PERFECTLY AND IT HAPPENS ON PURPOSE. BE AWARE OF IT.

MAKE A GIFT FOR SOMEONE

To give is to receive. The pleasure of giving fosters abundance. It doesn't have to be extravagant or take a great deal of time. It could be a handmade card, a piece of origami, or a poem. It may be tangible or it may be kind words. You don't need to go to a store in order to give something to someone. Tap into your creativity. Think playfully. Make a gift for someone. It's immediately priceless.

Children are constantly making and giving gifts. Drawings and colouring are made and shared. It's a completely natural act for children. And everyone involved feels good about it. In virtually every office I go into, I'll see children's drawings and colourings at people's desks or adorning office walls. They may be from their children, nieces and nephews, or the children of friends. But they're always treasured. Keep the gift of creating and giving alive no matter how old you are.

SPOIL THOSE WHO LEAST EXPECT IT

Give frequently and freely. Spoil those who least expect it. You can start a wonderful new cycle of positive energy and goodness. Do something extra for the person who doesn't expect it. Enjoy it, and do it again for someone else. It's fun and positive. Repeat as often as you can.

Some people love surprises. Some people don't. Be sensitive to people's wishes, but you may want to find out first hand. Be fun, thoughtful and playful and surprise someone with a gift or a kind gesture. It may not seem like much, but it truly is.

INSTEAD OF LOANING A BOOK, GIVE IT TO THAT PERSON

I love books; I always have. They represent knowledge, entertainment, escape and adventure. One of my greatest experiences was having the opportunity to go through the library of historical literature at the University of Dublin in Ireland. Over 200,000 books line the shelves that run from floor to vaulted ceiling. Many of the books are hundreds of years old. There is a thousand year old book on display. The room was alive with wisdom and history. It was palpable, moving and inspiring. Books possess magic. They are personal. Stephen King explains in his book, *On Writing*, that by no other means can a person (writer) have a thought and communicate it with perfect clarity to anyone, anywhere, in an instant. The individuals need not meet nor live at the same time. But the connection between them is perfect and timeless.

Over the course of a few years I amassed a fair-sized library of inspirational books in my office, from spirituality and religion to self-help and motivation. I enjoyed loaning the books to my co-workers. Eventually I decided I was going about sharing in the wrong way. I decided instead not to loan books, but to give them away. I created a library in the purest sense, without sign-outs or due dates or even expectations. The intention was to freely share knowledge and inspiration.

An interesting thing happened. People continued to take the books. Some were kept and passed along while others found their way back to the shelves in my office. But people began to bring more books into my library. The more

I freely gave away, the more that came into my possession. I was experiencing the magic of selfless giving and abundance. I had believed in the notion, but here it was, reinforced in no uncertain terms. I may have learned more from witnessing that abundance than all the information contained in all the books that were circulating through my life at that time. Let my experience be a powerful lesson. Instead of loaning a book, tape or CD, give it away. If owning it is that important to you, replace it.

GIVE WITHOUT EXPECTATION

The only great gift is that which is given freely and unconditionally. Give selflessly, without expectations. Those that give more will generate more for themselves in return, but only if that expectation is not part of the giving. Give solely for the joy of giving. Give for no other reason but that it feels good and spreads goodwill.

GIVE GENEROUSLY AND ACCEPT GRACIOUSLY

Give frequently and give generously. Give for the pure joy of giving. And when people thank you, say "You're welcome." Don't make light of giving. When you give, let the recipients have the opportunity to express themselves. We're too quick to say, "It's nothing" or "It's my pleasure." Allow the recipient to express their gratitude. Don't take away from the exchange. Everyone benefits. Keep giving. Don't do it for the thanks, but when someone is thanking you, take time, let them share their feelings, and enjoy the response. Saying "You're welcome" is an important part of the process.

ENJOY THE SUCCESS OF OTHER PEOPLE

Celebrate the success of others. Let other's joy be your joy. Feel their jubilation in you. Success, like all acts, generates momentum, self perpetuates and creates abundance. Do your part and take part. Enjoy the success of others.

There's comfort in familiarity. We like routine, habits and rituals. TV series like "Cheers" and "Friends" owe much of their success to the viewers desire to be part of the gang "where everybody knows your name" and to have a supportive group that we know we can count on. But great friendships are built, and like any structure it must be reinforced. Add to your friendships. Expand your circle of those you know, like and trust. Meet new people. Encourage new friendships. Celebrate life and celebrate with new people.

SHARE WHAT YOU WANT TO HAVE. GIVE AWAY WHAT YOU WANT TO EXPERIENCE. THE ATTITUDE OF ABUNDANCE GENERATES MOMENTUM AS IT PERPETUATES MANIFESTATION.

Changing the World
Around You

"We make a living by what we get, but we make a life by what we give."

"When you feel grateful, you become great, and eventually attract great things."

"Great things are done by people who think great thoughts and then go out into the world to make their dreams come true."

ASK SOMEONE, "WHAT'S THE NICEST THING THAT'S HAPPENED TO YOU TODAY?"

We waste time on negative thoughts and negative conversations. We replay things in our minds we wish we had or hadn't said or done. We mentally chew out people who we feel have wronged us. We remember the person who pushed in front of us or was rude to us. We go over these thoughts again and again, carrying them with us. It's time to break the habit.

Be aware of your thoughts and actions. Everything you do entails a choice and requires a decision. The choices you make will lead in one of two directions. Every thought you have and every action you take will either move you closer to your goals or further from your goals. There's no neutral. Doing nothing moves you further from your goals. Be aware of the power of every choice you make and keep moving along the path that takes you closer to your goals.

An effective way to do this is by catching yourself when you feel negative energy bubbling up in you. Know that it's okay, but process it and make the choice to continue along your positive path towards success. Do not initiate or facilitate negativity. This isn't always easy. When office commiserating or gossip starts, don't take part. Break the momentum or move on.

You can start a great conversation or derail a negative conversation by asking someone, "What's the nicest thing that's happened to you today?" For some it will be easy and natural to respond to this question. For others it may seem impossible. Don't rush any answers, let it flow. You may have to repeat it. You may be met with scorn. Don't worry about it. By asking the question you are moving closer to your goals and hopefully moving others closer to theirs. All in all, you will be doing good, making a difference and contributing to improving the world around you. So, "what *is* the nicest thing that's happened to you today?"

SEE PEOPLE FOR WHO THEY
ASPIRE TO BE. SEE PEOPLE FOR THEIR
POTENTIAL AND CAPABILITIES.

ENCOURAGE POSITIVE ATTITUDES

Actions are stronger than words. Behaviour denotes the type of person you are. Think positive. Be positive. Share it with the world around you and let it radiate. Let it flow through you, out from you, and back to you. Keep sending it out. You don't have to preach or get on a soapbox, but encourage what's positive. Let it come through your words and through your actions. Encourage positive attitudes.

BUILD PEOPLE UP

You can do great things by building people up. I don't mean hollow accolades just for the sake of praise. But be aware of the good things people do. It can be small things but if it makes a difference and it's valuable, let people know. You can make a good, positive person even better and you can turn a negative person around. All energy has momentum and the only way to stop the slippery slide of negative energy is to drive a wedge of caring in its path.

A friend explained to me that when he worked on trains, they could stop a rolling box car on its tracks by quickly jamming a small piece of wood in front of the wheel. See yourself as that rail yard engineer putting a quick stop to someone's negative energy with a positive thought, word or gesture. Help to get the people around you on the right track and let their positive momentum keep them there.

NEGATIVE PEOPLE CAN'T INFLUENCE YOU, ONLY YOU CAN

Nobody can truly influence you without your permission. Never doubt this. Only you are able to influence how you feel. Be aware of what's happening when you're bombarded by negative energy. It's going to happen. But it doesn't have to affect you. In his writing, Wayne Dyer explains how he handles negative thoughts. He simply sees it for what it is and says "Next!" to himself. He recognises it and lets it roll right off. You just happen to be in its path. Stand aside, say "Next!" to yourself and move on to the positive. That's where you belong.

In dealing with negative people, I draw from Star Trek, being the geek that I am. I simply say to myself "Shields Up!" and envision a powerful force field around me that's impenetrable by negative energy. I also use my 'Shields Up!" technique to mentally protect myself from cold and flu viruses. If anyone around me is sneezing, coughing or generally looking for a sickness sympathizer I don't have to be rude or confrontational. I don't have to lecture anyone on how to behave or how to be healthy if I don't care to. I don't have to run away either. I can still have a relatively pleasant, yet quick, interaction with someone who's negative. In my mind, my positive energy flows easily and strongly through my mental force field, but the negative energy simply dissipates. Try it. Find a mental system that works for you and keep negativity at bay.

THERE WILL ALWAYS BE PEOPLE WHO TEST YOU AND THAT'S OKAY

To improve the world around us, all we need to do is be positive and loving, be aware of feeling or behaving negatively, and change it for the better. That's it. All the other stuff will fall into place accordingly. Be prepared for negative people who will try to spread bad energy. They will test your strength and they will test you. Don't be afraid of it and don't be hurt by it. It's never personal. Just know that you're being tested. Be positive, strong and confident. This is your study. With this preparation, you can pass any test.

You can even be thankful for such tests. It provides opportunities for you to reinforce your strength, and rise above challenges that come your way. These tests are like exercise. Through training and repetition you become stronger. Relish the opportunities to get stronger. Be aware of the tests, and treasure them, knowing that you are better because of them.

FOCUS ON UNDERSTANDING EVERY POINT OF VIEW

The only differences that exist between us are those of perception. We believe people to be different because we view them differently. Overcome this by breaking down perceived differences. Work at understanding every point of view. It may mean reading different gospels, watching different movies or programs, listening to other opinions and asking more questions. By changing our perception and focusing on understanding every point of view, we can dissolve differences.

GO TO A FOOD MARKET WHERE YOU DON'T SPEAK THE LANGUAGE AND BUY SOMETHING YOU'VE NEVER BOUGHT BEFORE

This may not be easy or even possible for some people to do. Depending on where you live, you may not have access to a wide array of culturally different foods. If not, work with what you have available. Look for something you aren't familiar with or something you've never tried before. Try it out. You don't have to make it part of your regular diet. You may not like it. So what? Treat it like a cheap getaway to an exotic place without the hassle of airports or customs.

If you can find a different cultural food market, make a point of going. Stumble through the process, discover something new to try, and buy it. It'll give you the opportunity to experience life the way many people around the world do. Adopt the habit of experiencing activities that may not come easily to you. Position yourself on the other side of a cultural fence and learn what it means. Open your mind, your heart, and really experience it. It'll probably be uncomfortable. You may not feel treated well. You may encounter impatient people who are unwilling to find common ground. That's good; learn from it. Go through the process. The differences you may experience are only perceptual. But you may get a glimpse into a range of different perceptions at the same time. Open your mind. Be patient. Embrace what you may see as differences. Know that's all it is and we're really in the same boat, our routing may just vary a little.

Even at your regular grocery store, trying a piece of fish or fruit you've never had before is a great way to open up to new things and experience something for the first time. It can be very simple. I was recently going through the checkout at a local supermarket. I had some small red bananas from the plantain family. The young man bagging my groceries asked what they were. I told him. "Hmm, weird", was all he had to say. I liked that. I don't mind the label if that means I'm experiencing something unique. I was glad I hadn't bought the smelly durian fruit I'd seen in the store before. I'm not sure what he'd have said.

Fish is another great way to try something new. Usually the people selling it can give you some help on how to prepare it. Give it a try. Imagine you're on vacation, exploring exotic new places. You don't have to spend a lot of money. You may want to have something else handy for dinner just in case. But have fun with it.

FORGIVE

No matter what's happened, forgive. You will have greater peace because of it and you will move closer to your highest self. Without total forgiveness, we will always carry the weight of resentment or remorse. Let it all go. Look deep within and look beyond. Rise up. You're past it all.

Forgiveness, like love, is one of our greatest powers. Not a power over someone, but the power of goodness and enlightenment. It is not always easy. It may take years, it may require help, but without forgiveness we limit our potential. And it's a limit that need not exist. We are designed to be limitless. Don't let the baggage of blame burden you. Whether it's someone in your family, someone close to you, someone you just encountered, or yourself, start forgiving. Let it be a part of who you are. It'll get easier and it'll give you great strength. It's part of your path. Forgive.

SEE PEOPLE AS YOUR PEERS

Kids on the playground say "You're not the boss of me!" How true. I'm also not the judge of you, nor is anyone ever in the position to judge. I'm not talking about the legal system here. I'm talking about being judgmental. Judging requires labelling, categorising and creating differences that don't exist. We're all the same at our highest level of being. Work to eliminate judgement from your perspective. Start by seeing people, all people, as your peers.

One of my best friendships is the one I have with my boss. The only thing that kept the friendship from being as good as it is was my perception of differences between us. I saw him as "the boss" which created a whole host of issues that affected my ability to be myself around him. I realise that he, too, would like nothing better than not to have the label of "boss". It affects how people treat him and undermines the development of a lot of relationships. Treating everyone as a peer not only eliminates judgement, but frees you to be yourself. Be open and honest with people. Respect everyone, but remember that we're really all the same.

APPRECIATE RELIGIONS AND PHILOSOPHIES

Like language and culture, religion and philosophy are the greatest contributors to the perception of differences between people. Throughout history, these are the things most responsible for fear, hatred and war.

By appreciating religion and philosophy, all religion and philosophy, we dissolve differences and blur the lines of distinction. Virtually every religion and philosophy strive for the same things; enlightenment, peace, connection, eternity, guidance, love and happiness. The means to the end may vary, the labels may vary and the interpretation of the path may vary considerably, but the concept and the end goals are not that different.

You don't have to understand every belief. You don't have to agree with every interpretation. But appreciate it all. Differences in labels and interpretation don't make them wrong, it just gives the appearance of difference. Many are unwilling to recognise the value in all perspectives. So be it. But you can be above it. See labels and interpretations for what they are. You don't have to agree. But appreciate religion and philosophy. Every new perspective you encounter and every new opinion, including your own, just may be right.

PRAISE NEGATIVE PEOPLE YOU ENCOUNTER

Light eliminates dark. Love conquers fear. And kind words and actions will overpower the negative without fail. Try praising negative people you encounter. You will have to work harder, but make it sincere. They may love it. They may resent it. They may not get it. Some will and some won't. That's okay. The fact that some will get it and some will change for the better as a result of your actions proves it's worth it. Make the difference. The power is within you. Praise negative people you encounter.

HOLD DOORS

Hold doors for people. What's the worst that can happen? You're held up for an additional 10 seconds? More people get through the door than you'd intended? You feel taken advantage of? You can see how ridiculous that is, but it's the way we think at times.

Kind acts improve the world. The simple ones are just as powerful as the big ones. It's all good and it all helps. This is an easy and effective one. Hold doors. You'll probably end up making eye contact, sharing a smile or a "Why, thank you!" That's not why you do it. That's just a bonus.

SAY "GOOD MORNING"

I like "Good morning!" very much. It's descriptive. It's somewhat instructional and directive. It's positive. It's not dependent on anything. You make the statement with conviction and that's exactly what it becomes, a good morning. If some joker gives you "What's so good about it?", you have a great opportunity to explain exactly why it's a good morning. There's going to be weather (sun is warm and cheerful, rain is good for plants and trees, wind keeps the clouds away, snow is fun to play in); you're likely at a job (which you should be thankful for); you may have good health, family and you're alive! And that's just a primer list for novices. You can share all the great reasons you can think of for it being a good morning with anyone who questions you. Now that makes for a good morning. Some people won't even respond. That's okay too. Once you make the statement, you make it so. Say "Good morning!" Believe it. There, now it is.

SAY "HELLO" TO PEOPLE ON ELEVATORS

Comedian Stephen Wright tells a joke where he says, as kids, they would stand closely together, not speaking, just looking forward and up. He said it was his family's way of getting them to practice for riding elevators.

I'm not sure how it started or when it became standard protocol, but I don't understand the common practice of non-acknowledgement on elevators. Go on and get out on the skinny branches. Say "hello" to people on elevators. Some will think you're weird. If being friendly and open means being considered weird, then I'm willing to be weird. I can appreciate that some people may prefer to be quiet or keep to themselves. I'm also willing to risk making some feel uncomfortable. It's a risk, but I believe it's worth it. The benefit outweighs the cost. Open up. Spread some kindness. Say "hello" to people on elevators.

PLAY WITH CHILDREN

Children are a direct link to pure love. They're closest to the source of creation. Those who are spiritually enlightened see God in children's faces. To be childlike is to be without judgement or ego. Child's play is unadulterated, pure potential. Children come into this world without limits. We try to get back to this state of purity through prayer, meditation, books, courses, adventure and travel. You can tap into this by going directly to the source. Cut out the intermediaries. Have fun and learn while you're at it. Play with children.

> IT'S DIFFICULT FOR SOMEONE
> TO BE NEGATIVE WHEN THEY'RE
> INUNDATED WITH KINDNESS.

BUY A BOUNCY RUBBER BALL
AND GIVE IT TO A CHILD YOU DON'T KNOW

I've had wonderful experiences doing this. I've always enjoyed playing with those small, extremely bouncy balls made of dense rubber. They're usually called super bouncers or something similar and always come in a rainbow of fun colours. You can have a great time with nothing more than one of these balls and some concrete or a wall. You can enjoy them by yourself or with any number of friends. But one thing is for certain, you can spread a great deal of joy by giving these little things away. The pleasure they bring far outweighs the nominal cost. I enjoy buying one, playing with it for awhile, and then giving it to a child I don't know. Make sure they're not too young for the toy and you may choose to do it in front of the parent(s) so everyone feels more comfortable.

I find this a great opportunity to spread some joy, share some fun, and remind a few new people what a kind, abundant world we live in. You can play the part of Santa anywhere, anytime of year. Do it for the fun it brings, and enjoy the pleasure of it.

CHILDREN SHOULD BE SEEN
AND LISTENED TO VERY CAREFULLY

Children can be our best teachers, reminding us of simple times and simple pleasures; to make believe, run, laugh and play for the sheer joy of it, because it's our natural state to do so and to have fun using only our imagination. To draw, colour, paint and to make things. To sing out loud and not worry about what anyone thinks. To see all people equally and to not judge. To include everyone and share. To play and eat and rest completely, without stress or worry. To know things are okay and live fully in the moment. To take great delight and feel wonder in nature and everything around you. To believe and never doubt. To love unconditionally and be like our heroes. Children could lead us. Children should always be seen and should be listened to very carefully. For they say what they know and what they know is true.

LET YOUR ACTIONS
MAKE A POSITIVE DIFFERENCE.

AFFIRMATION QUESTION

What's the nicest
thing you've done for
someone else today?

APPLICATION EXERCISE

What's one thing
you can do, right now,
to improve your
relationships with others?

Write it down as a
goal for yourself. Set
a deadline for doing it.
Commit to doing it.

It could be an act of kindness to someone you care about, or sharing your feelings with that person. It could be making a call or writing a note to a friend. It could be preparing a meal for someone, giving a little more, or simply being patient with others.

In Chapter 8 (Laughter and Play), the *Wonderful Magical Words That Work*, "Don't Keep Score" have influenced me in a particularly powerful way. The more I thought about the significance of this statement, the more I realised it also holds true with respect to our relationships with others. Don't keep score. Too often we keep a mental tally of who has done what the most, or most recently, etcetera, in a relationship. I feel too much has been written about the "emotional bank account". This is the concept that we make withdrawals and we make deposits in our relationships. Acts of kindness, giving and generosity are considered to be deposits, while acts that are beneficial exclusively to yourself and therefore selfish, are considered to be withdrawals from the emotional bank account. I disagree with the whole concept. The idea of an emotional bank account, by its very nature, is based on the concept of scarcity. If you keep track of emotional deposits and withdrawals, you're keeping score, and I believe that's counterproductive to a healthy, sharing relationship. There's always going to be give and take, that's part of the balance that comes when two entities come together as one, but a harmonious equilibrium in fact can build something much greater than the sum of its parts.

Keeping score inherently perpetuates the notion of a winner and a loser, or at best a zero sum game. It denotes the concept of getting a bigger piece of the relationship "pie". I don't buy it. I don't believe that there is only one pie. I believe that in relationships, as I do with respect to money and life, that we have access to an endless supply of ingredients from which we can make an infinite number of pies.

Give of yourself because it feels good. Give to your relationships. Be kind, considerate and loving. Look for an opportunity to be generous because it's the good thing to do. It will come back to you, and you'll actually receive more once you don't expect it.

One of the most powerful, mutually advantageous behaviours to bring to a loving relationship is that of patience. Just be patient with your loved ones. Don't anticipate; eliminate expectations; stop keeping score, and forget about deposits and withdrawals. Just be kind, loving, and most importantly, be patient. I guarantee it will free you, empower you, and enable you to be a better partner, parent or friend, which will in turn facilitate a better, more loving environment for your loved ones, thereby making them happier and wanting to give more back. Everybody wins!

I appreciate that some people will find themselves in extremely difficult or abusive relationships. I hope that my suggestions to create self-empowerment and take positive action to improve your life will provide the courage and conviction to get out of a dangerous situation.

BEAUTY IS NOT WHAT WE ARE TOLD IT TO BE,
BUT WHAT WE DECIDE IT TO BE.

PART THREE	PERMANENT REWARDS: FOCUS ON LIFE

CHAPTER 7

Lessons of Enlightenment

*"Beliefs generate your thoughts
and emotions, which create your experiences.
To change your life, change your beliefs."*

— DICK SUTPHEN

"Things do not change; we change."

— HENRY DAVID THOREAU

*"You need not leave your room.
Remain sitting at your table and listen.
You need not even listen, simply wait.
You need not even wait, just learn to
become quiet, and still, and solitary.
The world will freely offer itself to you
to be unmasked. It has no choice;
it will roll in ecstasy at your feet."*

— FRANZ KAFKA

GET UP AND ENJOY THE MORNING

We were on vacation in Barbados at the start of the millennium. I would get up every morning before sunrise and sit alone in a lounge chair at the water's edge. It was the southernmost part of the island and I would face due east, looking down ten kilometres of sand and breaking surf to watch the sun rise.

Cumulous clouds on the horizon would slowly reveal the sun like curtains on a stage. Every morning was a spectacular show. Colour washed through a pastel spectrum while birds, new and exotic to my ears, regaled me with song from the cassurina trees nearby.

The feeling of communion with nature and creation provided me with peace and the courage to change my work. It meant less pay at the time but more freedom and happiness. I believed I could do whatever I chose to do. I'm sure I could have made my decision anywhere, but I know that the quiet time I spent at sunrise provided me with the courage, confidence and clarity to make it happen.

Morning is the time of day when we're most naturally in tune with creation. For thousands of years, people have worshipped the sun and its rising. It helps plants grow, it warms us and makes us feel good. The power of sunrise fuels morning prayer and morning meditation. Light is powerful energy. Light is also representative of pure love. There are now thousands of documented cases of near death experiences, all of which incorporate great light and with the light are peace and love.

By getting up early and enjoying the morning we remain close to the source of all that's good. Avoid using the snooze on your alarm clock and stop setting the alarm as late as possible. Sacrifice the thirty minutes of sleep if need be. Get in touch with the morning and you'll get in touch with creation.

GIVE THANKS EVERYDAY

Creativity and gratitude are fundamental to our existence. They're the basic elements of prayer and meditation. "Please" and "thank you" are some of the first things we learn as children or in a new language. "Please" and "thank you" represent manifestation (creation) and gratitude. Things come to us, and we are grateful. You can't have one without the other.

In the same way that we create what we want, we must also be grateful for what we experience and enjoy. Even as we experience challenges, we must give thanks, as life lessons will "open another door" for us or enable us to see what's truly important with greater clarity. Let "please" and "thank you" direct you in all that you do. Feel it at your very core. For all that comes to you, feel gratitude.

Gratitude perpetuates abundance. Give thanks for all you have, all you have had, and all you plan to have. Whether through internal appreciation, acknowledgement, prayer or meditation, give thanks. Appreciate everything, the good that we enjoy and the bad that we learn from. Give thanks throughout the day, everyday. Recognise your wealth and your abundance. Regardless of religion, give thanks.

LET YOUR INTUITION GUIDE YOU MORE.

SOAK UP YOUR SURROUNDINGS

Enjoy your surroundings, no matter where you are or how you feel. We're usually too busy or distracted to take note of our surroundings. But our surroundings offer up a rich gallery of beauty, stimulation and pleasure. Become aware of the bounty all around you. It's perfect and it's free!

I believe that we could package up where we are (where we live or where we work) and put it on display in Southern California or Florida. We could charge a high price and we'd line up to get in, marvel, take pictures, even buy a video of it from the gift shop and tell our friends they really must go.

But we see the same thing everyday, and we forget how spectacular our surroundings really are, right now, just as they are. We see it but we aren't aware of it. We don't experience it. But it's easy to change. Take a good look at the view through the window. Take notice of plants and trees. If you look out to high-rises, appreciate the magnificence of their construction. Step out from behind the lens you currently see through; rub your eyes; open your senses, and soak up your surroundings. You're in a wonderland!

EMBRACE SILENCE

Silence is always in short supply. As anyone living in a city knows, we're bombarded by more noises that we can even identify at times. Dr. Seuss's Grinch understood, "all the noise, noise, noise, noise!" We must create silence for ourselves. Find a place or make a place where you can go that is quiet. In silence we find spirituality and peace. In silence we find joy and love. Silence enables us to get into the creative gap and manifest all that we wish to be and have.

Silence is as imperative to us as light is to plants. Treat it as the food that it is. Relish it. Embrace silence. It will take time for your mind to get comfortable in the silence and it will do everything in its power to create noise. That's okay, let it. Just slowly turn down the volume. Eventually, you'll be able to turn the volume off completely. Reduce the noise and embrace silence.

Develop the habit of simply sitting quietly for a while everyday. This will eventually enable you to attain a level of silence and peace. It's an effective form of meditation. It will rejuvenate you. Don't fight the busyness in your head and the thoughts and voices that fill the space. Just be aware of it. It's not your innermost, true self. The chatter will eventually dissipate and leave you in the richness that is you. Be patient. You can manifest or you can just be. The choice is yours. Enjoy the silence.

JUST LISTEN

Sitting quietly and listening is an effective way to gradually create a silent environment. We usually try to fill the silence by talking, verbally or internally. Take time to just listen, wherever you are, and you will tap into a new sensory realm. More will open up to you just by listening.

We learn more by listening than by speaking. Speaking by its very nature is repetitive. We either say what we've heard or read, or share thoughts that already exist in our head. It's all, therefore, old news. We can't learn anything by talking. Listening, on the other hand, is how we learn, in addition to reading or experiencing.

Remember to spend more time listening. God gave you two ears and one mouth. God knows best. It's easy to remember the two-to-one ratio. Just count your ears and your mouth and use them in the appropriate, God-given ratio.

STOP AND THINK

Stop and think. It doesn't even have to be about anything in particular. It could just be some mental rest and relaxation, or the break could give you the opportunity to find new solutions to issues or gain perspective and insight. But the only way to foster these opportunities for calm and clarity is to relax your mind.

FEEL THE BEAUTY AROUND YOU

Beauty is all around us, in everything we see if we choose to see it. Beauty is not what we are told it to be, but what we decide it to be. See the beauty in simplicity.

Tap into the essence of all that's around you. Know that everything is beautiful and that you are part of it. It flows along with you and through you. Feel the beauty around you.

Children are full of wonder and beauty. Children laugh, play and grow as they learn. Learning is discovery and this represents change and ongoing development. Learning and discovery empowers youthfulness. Be young. Be as a child. Explore.

BE PATIENT

Reducing our dependence on time literally slows its passage for us mentally and physiologically. Being patient is one of the most effective means of dissolving the importance of time. You will reduce the chatter in your mind and become more aware of the beauty around you. You will develop better, richer relationships. Give others time to think and respond. Let people complete things around you. Give yourself a chance to just be. Be patient.

TAKE TIME

What's the hurry? We impose time-bounded restrictions on ourselves. We focus on the clock and the passage of time. It's counterproductive. Think of a time when you felt joyful, immersed in love or beauty. We say "time stood still". That's how we describe capturing a perfect moment. There's perfection in the absence of time. You can create those perfect moments whenever you want. Take the time.

The world moves at just the right pace. We can't control it. You can't make the world spin faster. You can't make the sun rise quicker. You can't get nature to hurry up. You're a perfect part of nature. Take your time. Do things deliberately and leisurely. You will marvel at your ability to accomplish many tasks effectively.

Nature moves along at the perfect speed. No point in telling the tide to hurry up. We can learn a lot from nature and the world around us. True, some people may actually move quicker than others. I suppose there's some cheetah that can run faster than 110 km/h while the others sit back and think to themselves "Man, can that cat move!"

Everything, including us, is moving at precisely the right speed. How many times have you made mistakes when you're rushing, because you're rushing? You have a perfect speed. Don't fight it. How often do you find yourself driving into a traffic jam or up to a red light just when you'd decided you were going to make up time? Don't fight the natural order of things and don't hurry the pace of nature. Accept what you can't change. Tune in, relax and slow down.

WATCH SUNRISE AND SUNSET EVERY DAY

Witnessing sunrise reinforces your creative ability. Like the sun itself, this part of your day can provide you with energy and the ability to grow personally and spiritually every day. Try meditating. Say the creative sound "ahh" as you start your day. You may choose to be, or you may send out your intentions of what you wish to have and to accomplish, and then let it all go. The universe will handle the details for you.

Sunset, too, will reinforce your connection with the divine. This time of the day is your opportunity to reflect and be thankful for everything in your life. Think of where you live, people you know and love, the health you enjoy, the food you eat, challenges and lessons learned. Give thanks for all. You may decide to meditate using the sound "ohm" to tap into the field of gratitude. Or you may take a moment for peaceful reflection. Enjoy memories. Learn from them. Then clear your mind for a sound, rejuvenating sleep to empower you for another wonderful day.

If it's cloudy, enjoy the dawn and dusk times of the day. But if you can let a sunrise or sunset hit you full in the face, soak it up. Know your creative ability and give thanks for all that you have and will have.

LOOK LONG AND SERENELY AT MOUNTAINS, WATER, TREES AND CLOUDS

Get to know the power of contemplation and meditation. The practice of meditation has been extremely powerful in my life. But getting a sense of peace and connection doesn't require lengthy or formal methods of meditation. Simply being outside and enjoying nature will accomplish a great deal in your pursuit of peace and happiness. Take the opportunity to be outside as much as possible. Take notice of all that nature has to offer. Look long and serenely at mountains, water, trees and clouds. Feel your connection with the beauty of the world around you and know that you are a perfect part of the universe.

It can be just a few minutes each day. Make the time to get out of your office for lunch or breaks. Step outside your front door or onto your balcony to start and end each day. This will also tie in with sunrise and sunset, associated with the manifestation and gratitude elements of prayer and meditation.

When you look at a mountain, think of the energy and time that went into its achieving the size and shape that you are witnessing. When you see water, think of the cycle of evaporation, condensation, clouds and rainfall. When you see trees, imagine the process of growth from a single seed finding nourishment in the soil, sprouting and turning light and water into food, strength and oxygen. Let the boundaries of time dissipate as you relax in the midst of nature. Breathe deeply. Stretch. Soak up the beauty of your surroundings and know that you're a part of it all.

WATCH BIRDS WHENEVER YOU CAN

Start to take notice of birds. We dream of having the ability to fly. Realise that a part of you is present in the flight of a bird. Visualise yourself swooping overhead, enjoying the view from above. Feel the air rush by your face and look out to the curvature of the Earth in your mind.

I find watching birds mesmerising. It's a great reminder of our connection with the sky and with nature. I marvel to think that many birds evolved from dinosaurs. If you're ever upset when your car's been "bombed" by a bird flying over, smile and be thankful that birds *have* evolved as much as they have.

Watch flocks of birds in flight. See how they dive and turn in prefect unison. That shows the perfection of nature. Birds don't need air traffic controllers or runways. They just fly, effortlessly, and they always get it right (except when confused by glass windows).

We can improve the manner in which we live by freeing our mind more and allowing our mind to flow. Try not to over-manage your life. There's perfect order to it. It just feels a little chaotic at times. Let your intuition guide you more. Get into the flow and enjoy the nature of your own flight.

WHEN WE'RE RELAXED AND
PEACEFUL WHAT WE NEED TO KNOW WILL
BE REVEALED TO US FLAWLESSLY.

SCHEDULE REST AND RELAXATION

Make sure you're scheduling time for rest and relaxation. We can fall into the trap of working extremely hard, then planning a vacation, and physically crashing when the vacation starts, even getting sick, because we've been pushing ourselves to our physical limits between vacations.

Get rest regularly and frequently. Use morning and evening quiet time, meditation, or exercise to rejuvenate yourself. Stay healthy, and let your vacation time be for fun, play, visiting, sightseeing or adventure. Let the vacation be a part of your schedule that makes you spiritually richer. Don't let the vacation be a necessity for your mental and physical health. Don't see regular rest and relaxation as a sign of laziness or weakness. Use rest and relaxation to make you happier, healthier and stronger.

Despite what you may believe, hard work is not required for you to be successful. It should be a natural and easy process. Balance your work with liberal doses of rest and relaxation. It's good for you.

IF YOU DON'T HAVE ENOUGH MONEY RIGHT NOW, YOU NEVER WILL

Think very carefully about these words. Don't think of them as negative. The statement is one of freedom. Stop chasing a moving target. It doesn't matter what you earn or what you own. What you have right now can give you a rich, fulfilling life. Your wealth is a function of your perspective and your openness to abundance.

You can have as much as you like, but you do, in fact, have it all right now at the most primordial level of your being. Stuff doesn't actually come into and go out of your life, it just changes form. It can change from the unmanifest to the manifest, but it's still just a change in form or order. It really is all here for you, right now. Only your perspective can change. So, if you don't have enough right now, you never will.

> THROUGH HARD TIMES OUR GREATEST LESSONS ARE LEARNED AND OUR GREATEST STRENGTHS ARE DEVELOPED.

STRIVE FOR INDEPENDENCE,
BUT KNOW YOU'RE PART OF EVERYTHING

Forget everything you ever believed about being different, separate or distinct. It isn't so. We're all part of the same stuff, at the highest spiritual level as well as at the subatomic level. We're all the same. We are nature and we are the world that we live in. Fear and ill will are impossible once you embrace this fact. Feel harmonious with the world.

While you're a part of everything, you remain spiritually independent, free to live as you wish and make all of your own choices. At times we may feel that others are calling the shots for us, and we are only players in the production of our lives, reading scripts that have been handed to us. This is not so. Know that while you're in harmony with the world around you, you are still your own boss. You are free to do as you wish. No one else controls you, and for this reason you are independent. It may take time to become comfortable with this, but it is unequivocally true.

TRUST

The Bible says "trust your neighbour, but tie up your camel". I say "trust your neighbour, and don't be so attached to your camel". The trustworthy trust. Live by the Golden Rule; to do unto others as you'd have done to you. Nothing else matters. Trust is a part of love, and love makes the world go around. Don't mess with the earth's rotation. Trust.

> EVERY THOUGHT YOU HAVE AND
> EVERY ACTION YOU TAKE WILL EITHER
> MOVE YOU CLOSER TO OR FURTHER
> FROM YOUR GOALS.

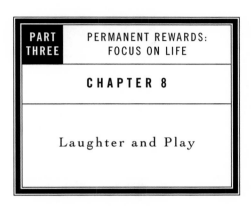

PART THREE — PERMANENT REWARDS: FOCUS ON LIFE

CHAPTER 8

Laughter and Play

"We are bound by nothing except belief."

— *ERNEST HOLMES*

"Each day, and the living of it,
has to be a conscious creation in which
discipline and order are relieved with
some play and pure foolishness."

— *MAY SARTON*

"When we seek money, or a good relationship,
or a great job, what we are really seeking
is happiness. The mistake we make is not
going for the happiness first. If we did,
everything else would follow."

— *DEEPAK CHOPRA*

SMILE AND LAUGH FREQUENTLY

Smile. I don't care how many muscles it takes to smile or frown. Smiling just feels good and the positive physiology perpetuates the momentum required for more good things. It's wonderfully infectious. Sure, there's plenty of science to back it up, but I'd rather go play. You don't even have to say "cheese". Just smile.

Laugh. The laughing Buddha had it right. Laughing dissipates fear. Laughing improves health. Laughing spreads joy. For years I thought the self help tapes I was listening to said the surest way to health, happiness and enlightenment was through medication. Turns out they were saying meditation. Ah, I know it's not that funny, but go ahead, laugh. It'll make us both feel better.

NAP WHENEVER YOU CAN

Napping is a wonderful, natural part of all animals' existence. We start our lives with frequent, regular naps and continue the habit for our first few years. But as school and work dominate our lives, the simple pleasure of napping gets ignored and forgotten, forced down the priority list as a result of other pressures and commitments either put on us by school, the workplace or ourselves. Our jobs may not make midday napping a realistic option, but think creatively. Many of us have flexible work schedules and home offices. We could easily work napping into our lives with a little effort and structure. Or perhaps you could nap after your workday. This would refresh you, make the evening more enjoyable and enable you to get up earlier in the morning. Try napping whenever you can and enjoy the benefits.

TAKE RECESS

I was driving past an elementary school recently at about 10:30 in the morning. The kids were out playing, having snacks and thoroughly enjoying the break. "Wow", I thought, "Recess!" It's a treasured part of a school kid's day, an opportunity for a snack, some fresh air, play and rejuvenation. How did we let that go? I know that somewhere early in middle school it becomes a "break" around the time that boys drop the Ys from their names and lunch kits are turned in for paper bags. It's all part of the process of "growing up".

But I believe recess represents all that's pure, healthy and natural from the school years of childhood. And I know we'd all be better off if we incorporated recess into our lives. Workplace monotony or stressful meetings would simply be put on hold for fifteen or twenty minutes while we take recess. I'm not talking about a smoke break or a coffee break. I'm talking about getting some fresh air, having a healthy snack, socialising and playing a little. That's recess. It makes sense. Start a recess break. I can assure you, you'll get good people on side. And for those who aren't willing to join in, well, you don't want to play with them anyway!

FEEL JOY

Light obliterates dark. Love vanquishes fear. Happiness, joy and bliss wash away all negative emotions. Simply feeling joy will make sadness and pain disappear. Like love, joy represents goodness, light and positive power. Feel the power. Feel joy.

Share what you want to have. Give away what you want to experience. The attitude of abundance generates momentum as it perpetuates manifestation. Keep feeling, experiencing and giving. Share joy.

Live in peace. Live happily. Live generously. Create and give thanks. Be joyful. Live joyfully. Feel happy. Radiate joy. Enjoy the richness of life. Never settle for less. Immerse yourself in abundance. Experience all that's around you and part of you. Live fully.

There is no price on love; no limit either. Take as much as you want and give as much as you can. Love is a perfectly thrown boomerang. Send it out with sincerity, passion and enthusiasm. It will always come back, stronger than before. Love with everything you have. Love completely. Love freely.

IT'S OKAY TO COLOUR OUTSIDE THE LINES

There are no final grades in life. Do your very best and enjoy it all. There's no judge and no contest. What you do will be perfect, no matter what. Design things as you wish. Use all the colours on your palette. Play, and remember, it's okay to colour outside the lines.

DANCE A LITTLE, EVERYDAY

Dancing keeps us young. Put on some music. Let it flow through you and move you. You can be all by yourself. If you're self-conscious, draw the drapes or blinds and indulge yourself. This isn't a dance contest. No one's judging you. It's just play. If you dance formally, I applaud you. But it can be easy and simple. Dance freely. Move your arms and your hips. Feel the music and dance.

GO BAREFOOT WHENEVER YOU CAN

When there's nothing between you and the world around you, you can't help but feel a greater sense of connection. Going barefoot is one of the simplest ways to enjoy this connection. Whether on sand, grass, dirt or asphalt, watch your footing, but enjoy the feel on your feet. They'll probably be a little tender at first. Do it as long as it feels good. Give yourself time to enjoy the sensation, and don't worry about getting dirty. Feet can be washed. Have some fun and go barefoot whenever you can.

HAPPINESS IS A CHOICE.

GET ON A SWING AND SWING AS HIGH AS YOU CAN

Don't take life too seriously. It was never meant to be a struggle. We all encounter hard times. Getting through them is part of the process of growing, becoming stronger and relishing the good times. We suffer at times in life, but life is not about suffering; it's just part of the dance. Play keeps things in perspective.

I was sitting on a beach in Perth, Australia on Christmas Day. The ocean mesmerised me; a blue deeper than I'd ever seen; almost violet. I was enchanted by the thought that there was nothing but this water separating me from Africa. I thought of the exotic romanticism I associated with the game of Risk as a child. I had found the island of Madagascar fascinating, and here I was—looking out to Madagascar across the Indian Ocean.

The wind was the strongest I'd ever experienced. The Freemantle Doctor, it's called, and I couldn't keep my hat on my head. I watched birds in flight along the water's edge. It took me a while to figure out why they were up in that wind at all. They would swoop at ridiculous angles, about ten feet off the ground, and then be thrown back a hundred feet at dizzying speeds before doing it again. It was like watching a cartoon. Their flight was actually comical. Then I realised they were simply at play.

We forget play is as natural as eating and sleeping. Remember to play and tap into your child-like state. By behaving in a fun, healthy, youthful manner, we remain fun, healthy and youthful. Play is the way to do this. Run, jump, skip, kick a ball, and get on a swing. Feel the air blow across your face and swing as high as you can. It doesn't matter who's watching or what anyone thinks. You might just give others the courage to do it as well. Explore, be open, be curious and play.

> WE ARE ALL CAPABLE
> OF BOUNDLESS CREATIVITY.

JUMP IN A PUDDLE

After all, that's what laundry is for. You can win the friendship of any number of dry cleaners this way, and I guarantee that the cost of cleaning won't come close to the amount of pleasure that you will derive from this retreat to childhood. And it's simpler than going to an amusement park; quicker, more convenient, no line-up and no parking issue. You just need a little co-operation from nature by way of some rain.

You may choose to be more cautious and test the depth before jumping in, but you do run the risk of watering down the whole experience (excuse the pun). The point, after all, is to abandon your reservations that come with "growing up" in order to remain wondrous, playful and child-like. You don't need to flirt with death or be reckless. Start with a good old-fashioned jump in a puddle. Don't be shy. And see if just once is enough.

GO FLY A KITE, SERIOUSLY

I can't help but wonder, if Ben Franklin happened to be out playing that day, flying his kite, and since it had never happened before, no one thought to suggest he stop in the thunder storm, or at least take the key off the string.

If there's a place near where you live where you can fly a kite, do it. You don't have to spend much money, a little kite will do. But do it. Kite flying connects you to nature in a wonderful way. No electrical power or batteries required, just you and the wind, with some string in-between. So, if someone tells you to go fly a kite, don't take offence. It's actually a kind and fun suggestion. Take them up on it. Fly a kite, seriously.

GET IN THE WATER, NO MATTER
WHAT THE TEMPERATURE AND SWIM NAKED

"This porridge is too hot!" "This porridge is too cold!"

I think those bears should be thankful they don't have to grub around for roots and berries like all the other bears!

Children will jump into water, no matter what the temperature, and play until their lips are blue. And they'll only come out when their parents get cold watching them. But I've had great times at a lake with friends who've spent more time trying to gauge the temperature of the water by looking at it than by swimming. "How's the water? Is it too cold?". Good grief! Now I'm not talking about "polar bear" swims either, but if the water is liquid and if it is not so hot that it's dangerous to your personal health, then get in the water!

Splash around and play a little. Have some fun. If it's not comfortable for you, you can get out, but try it. Experience it first hand. You can make up stories of bravado and endurance later on. And I'm all for skinny-dipping too. Never mind body weight, when you're naked in the water, you're still swimming "skinny". Don't break any rules. Careful not to offend. But if it's appropriate, enjoy the liberation and swim naked.

DON'T KEEP SCORE

I love to golf. Deb and I golf regularly. Sometimes I keep score and sometimes I play for the pure joy of playing. When I don't keep score I play better and I have a whole lot more fun. When I play with other people the question comes up, "What's your handicap?" meaning, "How do you usually score?" When I say I usually don't keep score, it's confusing to a lot of people. "How do you know how well you've done?" "How do you know who's won?"

As you can see, I'm not playing to "win" or to "beat" anyone. I love the game. I love to play, period. I don't want to get in on any betting that often accompanies play. I don't mind buying drinks after the round. But I just want to play, preferably with other people who love to play the game. Try playing for the pleasure of the game, whatever it is you're playing. A lot of games require some definition of victory and defeat, but most don't. Try it. Have fun and play.

LOVE YOUR PET

Pets keep us healthy, happy, and living longer. Having a pet is a wonderful way to feel and share affection. This perpetuates goodness and all that comes with it. I've seen people love and cuddle pets from cats, dogs and horses to birds, snakes and weasels. Pets are part of the family. The love that pets provide and foster is infectious.

I was given a small African tree frog as a pet when I was twelve. It was a bit of a novelty pet, one of a few that came into the pet department of our local department store. It lived in a small fish bowl of water, where it would float at the surface to breathe, and spent a majority of its time underwater, hiding amongst the aquarium rocks. I found frog food available at the pet store. I named him Steve. I know Steve was a "he" as he croaked, and I had learned that only the male of the species croaks.

By the time I left home to go to university, Steve had been my pet for eight years. People were amazed at how long I had had Steve. "How long do they live?", people would ask. I would always shrug. I figured Steve would be a part of my life for as long as was appropriate, nothing more, nothing less. He would give his high pitched croak every so often and I could make him stop by resting my finger against the side of his bowl. A simple relationship, really, not a whole lot of physical affection to be had, but I loved Steve and thought he was a great pet. He brought an element of fun and consistency to my life and I liked to believe that he was better off having "one square" a day in a pleasant, albeit small environment, safely out of the grasp of his traditional African predators.

I took Steve with me to university. The first time, we drove, I at the wheel, Steve in a jar. Later, we flew, I as a passenger, Steve in a jar in my carry-on. The security guard at the airport screamed as I passed Steve, jar and all, through the security camera area. Her screaming was very loud. Steve and I drew an uncomfortable amount of security attention as a result of the screaming. He and I were far more terrified than the security guard who, I must say, lacked an element of cool professionalism in the role. Fortunately, things simmered down quickly and Steve and I ended up having a very pleasant flight. There was no meal option for Steve as he was a non-paying passenger on my lap.

Six years later, Steve and I headed off to grad school, four thousand kilometres away. We drove. Late on the third day of the drive I was stopped for speeding. It was dark and the officer used a flashlight as he approached our car. I had my license out. Steve was on the dash in his travel jar.

The officer didn't seem to notice me, but kept the flashlight on Steve.

"You transporting live bait?", the young officer's voice came from the dark behind the light. The light stayed trained on Steve. I wasn't sure who he was addressing.

He repeated the question so I figured I better do the talking.

"Well, no officer, just my pet frog. His name's Steve." I figured a first name basis should break the ice. Maybe we could cop a plea.

"Where you coming from?"

I told him.

"There's been a terrible rash of Dutch Elm disease that's gone through the local trees."

I wasn't sure if that was accusatory, so I figured I better nip that line of questioning in the bud. "Uh, no problem there, officer, I'm from the West Coast and Steve is African."

No answer.

I wasn't sure where we stood. Apparently the elm disease was a real epidemic locally and was on everyone's minds. The officer finished writing up the ticket. The visit cost me $75. I felt that was fair.

Two years later, Steve and I finished grad school and came back home. I started working and Steve continued his life of swimming, breathing and occasionally croaking. I felt he was starting to show age.

One year later, after having been my pet for seventeen years (we don't know how old Steve was when we got him), Steve passed away. It was his time. I would still have to explain Steve to some people. Questions would come up and the novelty of him seemed to last.

Silly, maybe, but Steve was an important part of my life. He was there for my adolescence, my growing up, college, university, travel, relationships and jobs. I viewed Steve as a reference point, a reassuring constant while every other element of my life changed.

It doesn't matter how you define family; pets are an important part of who we are and the lives we live. If you can have a pet where you live, do. Life will be richer because of it.

IT'S OKAY TO EAT DESSERT FIRST

Let's not get bogged down in rules here. Have fun living. Get in touch with the child in you. Eat well. Exercise. Live healthy. Play more. And eat dessert first if you want to. Shake it up a bit. No one needs you to behave like "an adult".

I think part of growing up is hanging onto the best parts of being a kid. Playing fair, being kind, sharing, making new friends, laughing, singing and creating are some of the best parts of being a child, so hang onto them. Develop the habits of fun and play as part of your everyday life. Be responsible. You have a responsibility to yourself and those you love to be youthful and happy. Enjoy a treat when you feel like it. It's okay to eat dessert first.

> THE ONLY GREAT GIFT IS THAT WHICH IS
> GIVEN FREELY AND UNCONDITIONALLY.

PART THREE — PERMANENT REWARDS: FOCUS ON LIFE

CHAPTER 9

Now and Forever

"You are what your deep, driving desire is.
As your desire is, so is your will.
As your will is, so is your deed.
As your deed is, so is your destiny."

— *BRIHADARANYAKA UPANISHAD*

"Life is a promise; fulfill it."

— *MOTHER TERESA*

"Try then, today, to begin to look on all things
with love, appreciation and open-mindedness."

— *A COURSE IN MIRACLES*

SEE WHAT YOU WANT WITH CLARITY

Life is about choices. We perpetuate what feels good and we avoid what feels bad. We seek pleasure and avoid pain. We create the life we live. Things don't just happen to us. So go beyond wishing and hoping and decide. Decisively determine what you want with clarity. Repeat this to yourself, until the image is focussed and powerful. Think of your mind's eye as the world of make believe. But this is no imaginary game. That which you believe, and know, you make real. Child's play? You bet! Children know no limits on their own. It's the most powerful magic in the world. Thoughts trigger things and our decisions guide creative thoughts like a compass. So set your course. Decide, and see what you want with clarity. Nothing can stop you.

DO IT AGAIN

Choice is how we determine things. Change is how we improve. If something is not done right, change it, and do it again. There's no such thing as failure, only an unsuccessful attempt that represents an opportunity for new choices, change and improvement. Thomas Edison is one of the best examples of how repeated effort is the groundwork for success. In describing his attempts to create the electric light, Edison explained, "I never failed, I was simply unsuccessful 10,000 times."

Repetition is the mother of mastery and skill. We are creatures designed for consistent, ongoing improvement. If you've done something right, improve on it and do it again. If you feel you haven't done something right, change it and do it again. The only time we fail is if we stop trying to improve. Keep changing. Keep improving.

LEAVE YOUR WATCH IN A DRAWER FOR AN ENTIRE DAY

Get into the moment; after all, it's all we have. Our worries and stresses are time-based. We feel guilty about things that have occurred and we worry about things that haven't yet happened. By relinquishing dependence on time we can effectively nullify most concerns in our lives. Granted, certain things require knowing what time it is such as appointments and flights, but try a day without a watch; not just a vacation day either. It's extremely liberating. Then continue to increase the frequency with which you go without a watch or a clock. You'll find you get into a much more effortless pace, in tune with your body and the natural world around you.

In one of Deepak Chopra's audio programs he relays a true story of several miners who were trapped in a mine. Only one of those trapped had a watch. He called out the elapsed time to the others to help them focus on their potential rescue. What he secretly chose to do, however, was to call out that one hour had passed when in fact two hours had passed according to his watch. He in fact suspended time as perceived by the others. Upon their rescue, the timekeeper himself died. He had been acutely aware of the passage of measured time and what that meant in respect to the depletion of oxygen. All of the others in the group, who had not been aware of the "actual" time, were fine.

IF YOUR ACTION TAKES YOU CLOSER
TO YOUR DESTINATION OF JOY, REPEAT IT,
IF IT DOES NOT, DO IT DIFFERENTLY.

DON'T WATCH, READ OR LISTEN
TO THE NEWS FOR A WEEK

An American newspaper dedicated to only reporting good and positive news went bankrupt after only 3 weeks in publication. Good news, it seems, doesn't sell. I call this the "Chicken Little Phenomenon". All too often we waste time on perpetuating fear and worry. We worry about the stock market and the economy. We worry about natural disasters like floods and earthquakes. But none of these things are within our control. Any emotion expended on worry over such things is wasted energy. If you can control or influence something to change it for the better, do so. If not, let it go.

News coverage is probably the single greatest perpetuation of fear and negative energy. This is because the vast majority of news coverage is about things outside of our control and things that foster fear. Don't fall victim to the "Chicken Little Phenomenon". I appreciate that a lot of good work is done by people who report "the news". But I know my life is richer, happier and more peaceful by not allowing it to infiltrate my daily life.

News coverage is a business. It can interest us and inform us. But it comes with heavy distortion, based on how, where and when it is reported and by whom. Not watching the news for any period of time can be extremely freeing and liberating. Most of the things we worry about are outside our circle of influence. Concern over such issues is pointless. Don't watch, read or listen to the news for a week and see if it makes a difference. I guarantee the only noticeable difference will be positive.

DECIDE WHAT IT IS YOU TRULY WANT AND CREATE IT

Nothing can stand in your way, aside from you. You're in charge. You're the creation and the creator. God's within you and you're within God. I don't consider that religious or sacrilegious. The power to create and destroy, to give and to take away is intrinsic in who we are. Take the time to determine what it is that you truly want for yourself. Read books, listen to CDs, and go to seminars. Do whatever it takes! Don't make a big deal out of it. An element of privacy is important with respect to your goals. Don't flaunt it. Just do it and feel great about it.

Then keep doing it; change it; make it better, and do it some more. The world is yours.

MAKE A DIFFERENCE

You make a difference. Sometimes it may not feel like it. It's okay to feel down; it's natural to feel discouraged at times, but remember you're creating that emotion. Recognise it, and don't let yourself stay down. Think of it as a valuable reference point. Learn from it. Trust your intuition and leave the "down" behind. Relax and clear your mind. You'll know when it's time. You are an integral part of everything around you, therefore, everything you do makes a difference. Let your actions make a positive difference.

We need to feel that we are contributing and the world is better because of our being here. We need to feel worthwhile and valuable. We need to feel needed. Take charge and create this for yourself. You can be as needed as you need to be. Start doing a little more for those around you. Make it habitual and make it part of who you are. It can be selfishly motivated. If it feels good, do it. It's good to give and it's good to contribute. Keep doing it. Make a difference.

LET THINGS GO

You'll be well on your way in your pursuit of happiness and enlightenment when you're able to let things go. Let go of your attachment to things. It could be negative issues, resentment, ill will or bad habits that you've been hanging on to. Let them go. It could be attachment to material things. Let it go. Things come and things go. You have all you need with your ability to create right now. Don't get caught up in acquisition or ownership. It's all common property. Let it go. Whether it is opinion, argument, or ego, free yourself and let it all go.

LIVE YOUR LIFE AS IF IT'S FINITE
AND KNOW THAT IT'S NOT.

CHANGE YOUR HOPES, DREAMS,
WANTS AND ASPIRATIONS INTO DECISIONS

I have wonderful news. You no longer have to hope or wish for anything. You no longer need to want or have aspirations. Why? Because you can change all of these things into concrete, unwavering decisions. That's right. Decide what you want. Concentrate on it with passion and burning desire. Make it your definitive purpose, your reason for being. Feel all you want coming into your possession. See it. Know it. Then release and let it go. The universe will take care of the details. You can relax and leave the "work" to nature. Goods and goodness will come to you in perfect quantity and abundance if you truly want it to be so. And if you truly want it to be so, then change your hopes, dreams, wants and aspirations into commitment. Behave with conviction and devotion. Live with unwavering knowledge. Change your hope into belief and change your belief into action. Decide and it will be so.

REMEMBER

How often things come to us when we're not trying. When we're relaxed and peaceful what we need to know will be revealed to us flawlessly. So much of what we want and need to know is already there, waiting patiently for us to turn down the volume on our internal, infernal chatter. Whether it's a thought or a fond memory that makes us feel good, let your mind conjure it up and play it out across the screen of your mind's eye. Don't dwell on the past, but savour the good stuff. Let it fuel you and learn from it. The library of your mind is rich with memory, knowledge, solutions and ideas. Relax, clear the screen and let it play.

CHANGE YOUR HOPE INTO BELIEF
AND CHANGE YOUR BELIEF INTO ACTION.

TREAT LIFE AS A GIFT

Take nothing for granted. Take great pleasure in everything that you experience; the sublime, the mundane, the good and the bad. Our time is precious. Don't go through life on autopilot. Be aware of everything you do, make it all worthwhile and enjoy it fully.

Too often we view life as a chore, a burden that has to be endured or suffered. What an unfortunate weight to be burdened with. Life offers up challenges and hardships to be sure, but it has always been and will always be a gift of immeasurable beauty and value. Treat it as such. Say "thank-you" and try it on. One size fits all, batteries are always included and there's no best-before date. Treasure your gift. Treasure life.

Times may seem tough. They can be, but always remember that through hard times our greatest lessons are learned and our greatest strengths are developed. Know that whatever difficulties you face, it will be okay. Our darkest hours are before the light. Be strong. Hang on. Believe. It will always be okay.

Live this moment to the fullest. Soak up the richness and savour all that's around you. Life is a gift. Open it up completely, right now. Live in this wonderful present.

Learn from the past, and then let it go. Don't concern yourself with the future. What is the future but the ongoing present? It will always be out there. Live now. Be what you want, now. Do what you want, now. Your time is now.

> TAKE YOURSELF HIGHER,
> AND LIVE YOUR DREAMS.

AFFIRMATION QUESTION

What's the best
use of your time,
right now?

By this I mean, what's something you can do, right now, that'll make you happier, or healthier, or more successful, i.e. what will move you closer to your ultimate goal of success and happiness?

APPLICATION EXERCISE

What's one thing
you can do, right now,
to lead to a better life?

Write it down as a goal
for yourself. Set a
deadline for doing it.
Commit to doing it.

It could be promptly starting your work day instead of having a second cup of coffee and reading the newspaper. It could be repeating or rewriting your goals, focusing your attention on your objectives and feeling genuine enthusiasm about accomplishing them. It could be incorporating exercise or meditation in your life, or it could be increasing your awareness of the world around you, spending more time outdoors enjoying nature.

I was jogging along the seawall that serves as a breakwater to False Creek, an inlet of the Pacific that winds into the heart of Vancouver. It was a warm Sunday afternoon in June and the red brick walkway was busy with cyclists, walkers and other joggers. I was daydreaming, more aware of the sound of my breathing than my environment, when a sea otter emerged from the water and bolted up the steep rock embankment of the seawall, disappearing into some dense shrubbery several meters away. I'd never seen anything like it. The other people who noticed were equally taken aback. We had all presumably been in our own mental spaces, going about our activities, forgetting that even in the city we're still in the midst of nature.

I found this a powerful reminder. We can be in tune with nature wherever we are, at any time. Don't lose sight of the fact that the world we live in is rich with natural surprise, wonder and serendipity. You simply have to be open to it. If my head had been hung down or if I had been too deeply engrossed in my own thoughts, I would have missed out. How often are we missing out on witnessing the beauty of the world around us because we're not paying attention; we're not aware; we're engaged in mundane, repetitive thoughts? The otter scampering by enabled me to share a smile and a special memory with about half a dozen strangers and I believe we were all better off because of it. Open up to the world around you. Soak up nature and be a part of it. Beauty is there to be noticed and discovery awaits you.

I finished my run and slowed to a walk. I looked back, hoping to see more wildlife and was amazed to see how distant the bridge was that marked my halfway, turnaround point, that is, how far I had come. And I was struck by another powerful life metaphor. As you run along the path that is your life, maintain a balance of looking outward as well as looking inward. Set your sights on your ultimate goals; happiness, wealth, love, in other words, success, but ensure you continue to take progressive, consistent steps in that direction. Where you want to go may seem a long way off, but keep going in that direction. If it appears too far off and overwhelming, focus your thoughts inward and concentrate on making consistent strides and ongoing positive steps. And if you feel bogged down by the minutiae and the daily grind, look up, and visualise that ultimate destination that is your destiny.

When I look back at where I've come from, whether it's after a run or reflecting on life, I feel amazement, pride, and gratitude for how far I've come. My story, however, is not remarkable, nor is it unique. I would like that to be your inspiration. If I can apply simple strategies by way of *Wonderful Magical Words That Work* and live an exceptional life, filled with happiness and success, then you can too. I know that you deserve it.

LIVE YOUR DREAMS

I made up my mind, starting today,
I'm going to live my life in a different way.
I'm going to clear my thoughts at night
and sleep the night away.
And I'm going to live my dreams in the light of day.

I'm going to live my dreams.

I remember being warned: "Don't waste time on daydreams".
But those same dreams have all come true for me, it seems.
It the heart of every dream is a seed of reality
That manifests a better world for you and me, where we can

Live our dreams.

In dreams we rise above and know no boundaries.
You can make tangible what your mind's eye sees.
Never underestimate the power of your mind.
You can create your life and you will find that you can

Live your dreams.

CONCLUSION

I hope that you've enjoyed *Wonderful Magical Words That Work*. I urge you to read them again, a little at a time, each day. Answer the Affirmation Questions, which will keep your thoughts focussed on the positive. Revisit the Application Exercises, and write down your goals; set deadlines for their attainment, and commit to achieving them. Maintain this practise, adding new goals or modifying existing goals as you go.

Find the words that you feel fit with who you are and where you are going, and make them an integral part of your life. I leave you with three powerful quotes that I feel encapsulate much of what I have endeavoured to share with you. Take what you wish from this. Share as much as you can. And do everything in your power to live the greatest life imaginable. Namaste.

*"To accuse others for one's misfortunes
is a sign of want of education.
To accuse oneself shows that one's
education has begun.
To accuse neither oneself nor others
shows one's education is complete."*

— *EPICTETUS*

*"Change the things that can be changed,
accept those that cannot,
and have the wisdom to know the difference."*

— *REINHOLD NIEBUHR*

*"Go confidently in the direction of your
dreams. Live the life you've imagined."*

— *HENRY DAVID THOREAU*

BIBLIOGRAPHY AND READING LIST

Carlson, Richard. *Don't Sweat The Small Stuff.*
New York: Hyperion, 1997.

Chopra, Deepak. *Creating Affluence.* San Rafael: Amber-Allen, 1993.

Chopra, Deepak. *How to Know God.* New York: Harmony, 2000.

Dyer, Wayne. *Wisdom of the Ages.* New York: HarperCollins, 1998.

Dyer, Wayne. *You'll See It When You Believe It.*
New York: Harper Collins, 1989.

Dyer, Wayne. *Your Sacred Self.* New York: HarperCollins, 1995.

Fulghum, Robert. *Words I Wish I Wrote.*
New York: HarperCollins, 1997.

Fulghum, Robert. *All I Really Need to Know I Learned in Kindergarten.*
New York: Ballentine Books, 1986.

Hill, Napoleon. *Think and Grow Rich.* New York: Ballentine, 1960.

Irvine, David. *Simply Living in a Complex World.*
Toronto: John Wiley & Sons, 2004.

Jones, Laurie Beth. *Jesus, CEO.* New York: Hyperion, 1995.

King, Stephen. *On Writing*. New York: Simon & Schuster, 2000.

Robbins, Anthony. *Unlimited Power*.
New York: Fawcett Columbine, 1986.

Ruiz, Don Miguel. *The Four Agreements*.
SanRafael: Amber-Allen, 1997.

Sharma, Robin. *The Monk Who Sold His Ferrari*.
Toronto: HarperCollins, 1997.

Sharma, Robin. *Who Will Cry When You Die?*
Toronto: HarperCollins, 1999.

St. James, Elaine. *Inner Simplicity*. New York: Hyperion, 1995.

Tolle, Eckhart. *The Power of Now*. Vancouver: Namaste, 1997.

Tully, Brock. *Reflections for Sharing Dreams*.
Vancouver: Hay House, 1994.

Tzu, Sun. *The Art of War*. Oxford, 1963.

Walsch, Neale Donald . *Conversations with God*.
New York: G. P. Putnam's Sons, 1995.

Winget, Larry. *Profound Stuff*. Tulsa: Win Publications, 1995.

WONDERFUL MAGICAL WORDS THAT WORK

Like a magnet attracts steel, applying the secrets of *Wonderful Magical Words That Work* will perpetuate positive experiences for you, and you will see wonderful magic appear in your life!

"In Bill's book, every passage I read touches my heart and makes me want to share his message with everyone I speak to."

— DAN CLARK, RATED TOP TEN SPEAKERS
OF THE WORLD AND BESTSELLING CO-AUTHOR
OF *CHICKEN SOUP FOR THE SOUL*

WONDERFUL MAGICAL WISDOM THAT WORKS

The greatest masters of all time share with you how to lead a remarkable life in *Wonderful Magical Wisdom That Works,* enabling you to take charge of your life and live your dreams!

"This is a wonderful book full of wonderful words for a wonderful cause. Read it and enjoy!"

— BRIAN TRACY, BESTSELLING AUTHOR OF
MAXIMUM ACHIEVEMENT AND *SUCCESS IS A JOURNEY*

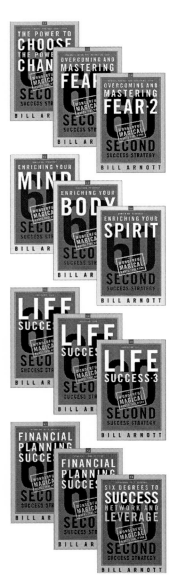

60 SECOND SUCCESS STRATEGY
PERSONAL DEVELOPMENT LIBRARY

 Realize significantly greater success and happiness in just 60 seconds a day! A complete 24 book set (21 unique strategies in 7 key areas of personal development), including 3 bonus books filled with Key Success Drivers, Application Exercises, and Success Tools enable you to apply simple exercises with profound, life changing results!

"If you want to move from where you are to someplace better, Bill's books can help you do that. Don't JUST read them — USE them and you will see better results and more peace and satisfaction in your life."

— LARRY WINGET, BESTSELLING AUTHOR OF
SHUT UP, STOP WHINING & GET A LIFE AND
THE SIMPLE WAY TO SUCCESS

QUICK ORDER FORM

____ copies   *Wonderful Magical Words That Work*
$19.95 Cdn + 7% GST + $2.50 S&H per book

____ copies   *Wonderful Magical Wisdom That Works*
$19.95 Cdn + 7% GST + $2.50 S&H per book

____ sets   *60 Second Success Strategy*
Personal Development Library (24 book set)
$199.95 Cdn + 7% GST + $7.50 S&H per set

Discounts are available for quantity purchases.

....
NAME

....
MAILING ADDRESS

....

....
CITY

....
PROV/STATE   POSTAL/ZIP CODE

(...............)..
PHONE

....
EMAIL

◯ Visa   ◯ Mastercard

                                            /
....
CARD NUMBER   EXPIRY

Thank you for helping our fund-raising efforts for Make-A-Wish Foundation and congratulations on making a difference!

Cheques payable to Wonderful Magical Publications

Orders can be mailed to Wonderful Magical Publications 409-15368-16A Avenue Surrey BC Canada V4A 1S9, phoned in (604) 542-4331, or emailed through the website at www.WonderfulMagicalWords.com

Contact Wonderful Magical Publications at (604) 542-4331 or www.WonderfulMagicalWords.com to book Bill Arnott for your own educational, enlightening, and entertaining seminars.

"Bill's positive energy & outlook on life is contagious and an inspiration. Everyone should be as fortunate as we were to experience his fun & engaging presentation."

— SONYA ORR, PRESIDENT, ROTARY, VANCOUVER

"To 'standing room only' crowds, Bill is funny, insightful and most of all, inspirational. One feels a sense of empowerment when he's through. At any cost, he is a must see!"

— BRAD CAMPBELL, REGIONAL DIRECTOR,
INVESTORS GROUP, WHITE ROCK